Her Eyes Were On India

Mary Ann Parfitt

Dedication

To my pen pal, Anju, whose friendship inspired this book.

Acknowledgment

My pen pal in India played a big role in the publication of this book. Her inspiration and encouragement allowed me the confidence to sit down and begin drafting this story.

Though the story and characters are fictional, made up in my own mind, I received information about the language, culture, and area of India from her.

Some of the conversations in this book are based on actual conversations we had during our email communication but are significantly altered to fit the storyline. This story is fiction.

I thank you, Anju, for your contribution to this book and to my life. You are a beautiful soul.

CONTENTS

About the Author

Mary Ann Parfitt was born and raised in Greensburg, Pa., where she still lives. She retired from a 30-year career as an office supervisor and began her writing adventures in 2022.

This is Mary Ann's third book, and in her opinion, her best book. She feels her experience has matured with each piece of writing.

She is active with many social groups, loves photography and traveling. Her dream is to write a bestselling novel.

I have met myself.

And I'm going to care for her.

Fiercely -

Glennon Doyle

Chapter 1 – Emily

"Gosh, I'm lonely," she said to Spot, her gray tabby cat, who was sitting on the kitchen windowsill while she gazed out and drank her coffee this beautiful Sunday morning in February. Valentine's Day always reminds singles they are alone.

She had just returned from church, changed into comfy clothes, and had no idea what to do with herself. The sun was shining on the patio, and Emily could see signs of life everywhere. It was going to be an early spring. Soon, it would be time to weed the gardens and plant more shrubs, a process she loved until fall when it became a burden again.

Spot showed little interest in the conversation, absorbed only in the birds building a nest in the oven air vent protruding out the back of the house. She could have had that vent removed during the kitchen remodel but did not have the heart to take away the space the birds had been using for a home since she moved in three years ago and who knows how long before that.

She glanced over at the puzzle on the dining room table, waiting patiently for it to be finished. She had lost interest.

Noticing the morning had ticked by, and her stomach

told her it was time for lunch, she moved to the fridge, opened the freezer section, and stared at the array of frozen food containers she had cooked in advance to pull out later when hungry for them.

"What am I hungry for?" she said aloud to nobody now since Spot had tired of the birds and moved on to batting a bell ball around the house.

Pondering over the available options, such as meatballs in sauce, chili, pre-grilled burgers, or hot dogs, she pulled out an individual container of chili and popped it into the microwave for exactly six minutes. She had done this before. Too many times.

"Oyster crackers would be good with these, but I don't have any. Butter bread will be just as good. I think I have some Italian in here." She looked around.

Talking to myself is becoming the norm these days. I really need to get out of the house.

She remembered how excited she was when she bought her house all on her own. Her career was moving forward, and she had done well establishing her credit, thanks to her dad's teachings before he passed. He had taught her to be a strong, independent girl from an early age. Now, at 32, she is wondering if she is too independent.

After moving in, except for work, she had not left the

house for three weeks, being absorbed in the sense of accomplishment. Remodeling and decorating had become a priority even though she was dating Steve.

Steve had wanted to move in with her as they worked on projects together, but Emily was not interested in living with anyone. As much as she appreciated his help, they had only been dating for a couple of months, and she had not fallen in love with him.

"This is my first time living on my own, and I'd like to take at least a year for myself," she told him when they talked about it. She had always had roommates after she moved away from home.

"I'm not willing to wait that long," he replied. "I am ready now. I don't see why we can't try it out. If it doesn't work, I'll move out."

Emily could see so many struggles with that idea and getting him out was the greatest struggle of all. He had a way of telling you what you wanted and did not listen to what you were saying.

"I just feel strongly about it. I think a relationship should be moving toward marriage. Living together is a big commitment for me. I do not take it that lightly."

Growing up Catholic, Emily had always struggled with her values of abstinence before marriage and premarital sex.

Her guilt was strong, and she would find herself in confession more often than she wanted to be.

"Forgive me Father for I have sinned. I am having sex outside of marriage."

"Do the best you can" would always be the reply from the younger priests, but the older, more seasoned priests would sound sterner, and the penance would always be greater. Because Emily was a Sunday school teacher, the emphasis for her was on living a moral life.

Steve was catholic, too, but it didn't seem to bother him as much. It is always different for men, in the church and in life.

"I know things have changed as far as how sexually active women are these days, but I do not believe that it is conducive to growth in relationships or marriage."

In fact, being a child psychologist and family counselor made her very conscientious about morality with young people, and she believed young people being sexually active is not conducive to the community and society overall.

The emotional level of a teen is not mature enough to manage what a sexual relationship does to a young person, boys, and girls.

"You put too much importance on religion. Things

are changing." He had been pushy once again, discrediting Emily's thoughts and feelings.

"The bond should be emotional first," she told him. "Not physical. A Physical relationship is not going to last forever if it does not have a good foundation of love and respect."

"You don't think we have love and respect for each other?" He asked.

She bit her lip. "Well, sometimes you don't listen to me or seem to understand what I'm saying."

"You're imaging that. I always listen to you." *Oblivious.*

In the end, Steve decided he did not want to wait and moved on to another woman who was more receptive to his way of thinking. And Emily was alone in her new house. That's when she got Spot.

A coworker came in one day complaining a kitten had been dropped on the road in front of her house and was now living under her porch crying all the time.

"I go out and give it food and water, but I do not want a cat in my house with the baby coming and all. Does anyone want it?" she had exclaimed in the employee lounge one day while they were having lunch.

"I'll take it," Emily said right away.

"Great! When can you come and get it?"

That day, Emily grabbed a box from the basement stock room, stopped at the store to buy a litter box, litter, and food, and then went to Casey's house to get the cat. When she arrived, Casey had caught the kitten, and it was digging full claw into her shoulder, shrieking for dear life.

Emily walked up onto the porch, grabbed her (turned out to be a girl) by the scruff of her neck, and immediately went into a fetal position. Once snuggled into Emily's neck and hair, she calmed down. At that moment, Emily became hers.

At home, when Emily bathed her, she discovered an orange spot on the top of her head, which is why she named her Spot. Spot became the most affectionate kitty, cuddling in the crook of Emily's neck at night to sleep and laying on her chest while watching TV.

She also became a strong, independent female, just like Emily. She would hunt and kill all the rodents in the neighborhood. Many of the neighbors would find gifts on their doorsteps and were grateful those rodents were not living in their yards and basements.

Emily would find offerings in her house too occasionally if she didn't be sure to keep doors and windows closed and repair all holes in screens Spot managed to claw through. The cat also loved rabbits as a meal, much to Emily's dismay.

She would sometimes find half-eaten rabbits on the porch and be completely freaked out about it. But otherwise, Spot was a good cat and Emily's favorite companion.

After Steve moved on, Emily decided to join some groups to meet new people as the old crowd had either moved, were married with kids, or had become workaholics.

Her life had become a routine of work, home, work. The worst of it was eating alone. Emily did not mind eating alone in restaurants. In fact, she sometimes preferred it. But she hated eating alone at home. It probably stemmed from growing up watching her mother eat alone.

Her mother, Anne, would always see that she, her brother, and their father were served first. By the time she sat to relax and eat her own meal, they had finished and left the table. Emily remembered watching her mother one day alone there eating, and she thought about how sad it looked.

Her parents, Joseph and Anne, did not have a close relationship. They did not hug, kiss, cuddle, or touch in front of the kids. Emily wondered if they did any of that in private and doubted it. In fact, she could not remember them ever showing their kids any affection either.

There wasn't much communication between any of them as well. If Joseph and Anne decided to do something that affected the family, they just did it, and the family was not consulted about it. No family meetings here.

When Emily was fourteen, a boy she knew who had a crush on her got her a collie puppy that she had wanted so badly. She was told she could not keep it because she wouldn't take care of it.

Two years later, Emily's dad decided he wanted to breed dachshund puppies. So, Emily was given a female dachshund. About six months later, Emily came home from school to find the dog gone.

"Where is my dog," she asked her mom.

"Your dad took her to breed," Anne said, and that was all.

A few days later, the dog was back. Not pregnant. No discussion. No explanation. That is how things went in Emily's house growing up.

Eating the hot chili with butter bread slowly, Emily opened her laptop and scrolled down her Facebook page to see if anything was going on. Nobody was posting anything.

"They are probably outside enjoying the beautiful

weather!" she said loudly to herself.

Emily saw an article online about Existential loneliness that said, "While some scholars see existential loneliness as something that can be appreciated positively." Researchers suggested that "one finds strength in being solitary, although it takes effort to realize this situation" and that having connections with others is crucial to a fulfilling life, as humans are social creatures. Dissatisfaction with life, lower self-esteem, reduced meaningfulness of life, and depression are all Potential effects of loneliness."

Logging out of there, she went onto the social group website to see if there were any events going on with the women's group she belonged to.

The Butterflies group leader, Mandy, made all the members organizers so anyone could schedule events, ensuring there would be something always going on. There was nothing going on today.

Emily thought about putting up a suggestion for walking but soon realized no one would see it posted this late in the day.

"Well, I'll just go for a run," she said, cleaning up her dishes and wiping off the table.

She pulled her long brown hair back in a ponytail, got her best running shoes on, and headed to Twin

Lakes Park in Greensburg. The upper and lower lakes had great trails along the waterline with paved stones.

There was a combination of open space and some tree areas, so you got a good mix of sun, where it was very warm, and shade that made the air very cool.

The lakes were connected by a wall and bridge, with an overflow that resembled a waterfall, making it a figure eight. When walking both lakes in that way, the distance was about two miles.

As Emily ran around the lower lake, up the steps, and across the bridge to the upper lake, she was aware that the falls had dried up since it had not rained in a while.

The trees were budding, and spring flowers were just coming up. A few people were fishing, and some were just walking.

She thought about the way things are today. Social groups are now forming online; Social events are now scheduled online. Any communication that happens on a phone is either via text or Messenger. These ways of communicating have their good points and bad, but whatever happened to talking on the phone or writing a letter and waiting weeks for a reply?

Remember how fun it was to get mail? It seemed like

personal relationships were not being deeply formed with this online way of doing things, Emily thought. There was no emotion anymore.

Emily remembered when she was in school, they had a Pen pal program. The students were assigned a person in another state or country and exchanged letters.

Emily did not participate in this program because, at that age, she did not know what to say to a stranger. But she heard the other students talking about their experience and how close they got with their pen pal.

Hm. I wonder what it would be like to have a pen pal now. And how would I go about finding one?

When Emily got home, she went right onto Facebook. She checked out all her online friends and picked out the three people who lived furthest away from her. She sent them each a private message that simply said: Would you like to be my pen pal?

Chapter 2 – Rishat

On February 14, the advent of Spring came, and Rishat would celebrate Saraswati Puja, the worship of the Hindu Goddess of Learning, and the patron deity of students and scholars.

Her daughter, Jaya, wanted to do this Puja, so Rishat made all the arrangements at home with Jaya's help in preparing the offerings. Rishat chanted the Sanskrit mantras (verses in praise). They dressed in yellow on this day.

Normally, one sits on the floor to do the puja, but in deference to Rishat's creaky knees and back, they sat on stools to perform the rituals. It had been many years since she participated in this tradition, but it came back to her quickly and easily as she went along. When they finished, Rishat felt some peace with the spiritual struggle she had been experiencing, but not completely.

The next day, Rishat's husband, Kumar, was celebrating his birthday. They were both working that day, he at school and she with her tutoring lesson, so Rishat cooked him a simple chicken dish with parathas, a kind of flatbread, at home, while Jaya made dessert, sugar-free oat pancakes with dark chocolate, bananas, strawberries, and honey. Jaya was always thinking of what was healthy for her parents.

Rishat was glad to have her daughter home for a visit from her first year at university. It would be a short visit for her before Jaya accompanies Kumar to visit his family in South India, quite far away from where they live in Ahmedabad. Rishat would also be glad to have some time alone when they left.

During the early years of marriage, they lived with Kumar's parents, helping to take care of them. They were a significant help to Rishat when Jaya was born, too.

But not long after Jaya turned five and started school, her in-laws moved to South India to live with Kumar's younger brother when he married his wife. They stayed with them as their family grew and became blessed with three children.

Since his father passed, Kumar wanted to spend more time with his mother. She knew the excitement he felt with his upcoming trip.

Last summer, before Jaya left for University, Rishat took her on a trip to visit her own family and old friends she had not seen in a long time.

She had planned for her daughter to visit Kolkata and Assam, both in eastern India, quite across from where they were on the west coast. She had looked forward to it and partly regretted it for different reasons.

"Why?" Kumar asked when she confided this with him.

"In Kolkata, I'll be visiting old school and university friends whom I haven't seen for ages. We were students when we were last together! We've kept in touch sporadically as you know, but I don't know quite what to expect now. I have changed a lot!

I wish to show Jaya the grand spectacle of the festival in Bengal and Assam. I'm excited about that, but in Assam, it's going to be meeting my parents' relatives, cousins, nieces, and nephews, even a few grand nieces and nephews that still live in Assam. I haven't seen them since 2015. So, we'll meet as many as possible in a brief time."

"It's a lot, I know. But it will be fine," that was all he said.

She didn't feel comforted. It would also be the first solo trip ever with her daughter. She felt like they were strangers for some reason. Rishat was not close to her own parents, and they had not been a source of support or encouragement when Rishat found she could not have a big family as they had hoped for in her marriage to Kumar.

And she wasn't sure she wanted to reconnect with

her roots. *They're nice, mostly,* she thought, and they had been urging her to come so they could spend time together and get to know each other.

It was for Jaya, who wished to meet her extended family and thought it'd be good for her and Rishat to reconnect with friends and family on Rishat's side. The last few years had been mainly focused on Kumar's family.

Preparing for the trip was stressful since she was not used to putting things together on her own, but the journey was worth it. Once she arrived and the ice was broken, she found herself enjoying the time and company. Jaya was even surprised to see this side of her mother, a laughing, fun woman she had not seen before. Rishat hoped Kumar's experience with Jaya would be just as gratifying.

Rishat realized how serious and strict she had been with her daughter to raise her with good values, but not having siblings had put all the focus and pressure on her.

Now, they were developing a different kind of bond between them. As Jaya was now grown up, a bond between woman and woman could develop.

Once Jaya left for university, Rishat found herself looking for stuff to do. Kumar being the Director cum principal of a school in Ahmedabad, Rishat got pulled in gradually as a "part-time consultant."

"No fee or salary? she had asked.

"No. You do not have the education to qualify, and we do not have the budget," Kumar said sympathetically.

It is not usual to have parents volunteering on a regular basis as most parents are working. If they take the trouble to show up and give their time and effort, they prefer to do it with remuneration.

She reluctantly had one or two initial interactions with students and teachers, but now, on popular demand, she was to go there at least twice a week to conduct workshops with them. She was not very willing to cut down on "me time," but also did not wish to say an outright 'No' when the teachers and students enjoyed their time with her so much.

"I will stay with you until I get bored," she told them, laughing. They'd assured her that they would not let her get bored!

Rishat loved kids. The fact that she could only have one child was a disappointment for her and Kumar.

When her marriage was arranged for her at 18, the decision was to have three or four children, starting immediately. Kumar wanted Rishat to wait before going to work.

To have a big family, the norm in India being one or two, Rishat would forgo college and give up education and dreams of teaching for this. But after Jaya was born, Rishat developed medical conditions that would not allow her to have more children safely. This kind of work was a way of fulfilling that maternal desire she was missing.

However, not having more children took a toll on her marriage. She felt disappointment coming from Kumar as, over the years, he poured all his energy into his job and the time he spent with Jaya.

They adopted pets to fill their lives and bring amusement for them, as well as companions for Jaya, two dogs, and a cat.

Now, only her dog, Cujo, remained. He was fourteen this year and had been diagnosed with early-stage kidney issues, so Rishat spent quite some time preparing his special kidney-friendly diet and persuading him to swallow his medication.

"He's not cooperative and struggles madly," she told Kumar. "Like I'm about to murder him (before) and then acts all weak and near collapse victim mode (after) while keeping an eye on me to see whether I feel guilty about torturing him! He's the complete drama queen!" *(King didn't sound right)!*

Cujo loved going to the new school with Rishat, so

they went for 'walkies' every day after everyone left campus, and when she had sessions, they went during school hours.

But now that Jaya was off to university and the family of pets was dwindling as well, Rishat was experiencing a significant emptiness in her life, though only 38 years old. At times, she felt crazy and wondered if she could have experienced a mid-life crisis already.

She thought of going back to school herself, finally, to get a teaching degree. Many women in India become private tutors, coaching students at home and helping them to complete school homework and prepare for tests like Rishat had been doing.

Now, she could get a real teaching job and get paid for her time. *But the cost of school, at this age, and Jaya's education now. Was it realistic?* She thought not.

Some of the friends she had made over the years were mostly through Jaya's classmates. The mothers of the other kids were usually jobholders, so the extent of the interactions had to do with school functions. Jaya was on the Cricket team all through high school. Kumar insisted on being at every game so Rishat would go along not really interested in it but supportive of Jaya.

Sports day at most schools invites parents. They set up snacks (fast food) and juice stands but were not served by parents, so Rishat did not even have a function there.

The school usually outsourced commercial fast-food vendors who set up stalls and made brisk sales. She really enjoyed going to these for that reason, getting away from her strict healthy diet to eat fast food for a change and watching the kids play.

However, Rishat did not feel comfortable being socially outgoing, so the relationships she tried to make were superficial. This lack of close, long-term friendships made Rishat think of a quote, "Good fences make good neighbors," as Frost said.

"I'm not naturally one to put up walls," she said to Jaya while watching her pack for the trip to see her grandparents. They were talking about what Rishat was going to do while they were gone.

"Why have you not kept in touch with the family and friends we went to visit last summer?" Jaya asked. "Have they not tried to stay in contact with you? You should go back and visit again."

"It takes a rare kind of humanity to extend yourself to others. If they don't want to put in time and effort to build a friendship, you're better off being you, not trying to please everyone always. It's a pity that the world seems overfull of mean persons who shut others out."

After Kumar and Jaya left for their family reunion trip, Rishat sat on the balcony of their apartment to reflect on the conversation. Sipping a cup of Masala Chai, she took out her journal and began to write her thoughts.

"It takes a lot to hold a marriage together, and it won't hold together unless we take turns to hold it together, is what I've found. One person can't do it alone.

"So, no matter how much he irritates me at times, to be fair, I'll have to give credit to my husband for being caring and agreeing with most of what I've wanted to do in life, and in general letting me feel that he has my back when the world gets too much."

This was what Rishat believed and lived by. So why now was she having such feelings of emptiness and things not fitting in with her life?

If her parents had not arranged this marriage for her, would she have just met someone else? Fallen in love? Would it have been better?

She thought of a friend from youth she had slowly lost touch with and now wondered if that friend was online. Grabbing her phone, she logged on to Facebook to see if she could find him.

There, in her message box, was a message from a Facebook friend from the United States. This woman had kept showing up in her feed years back with some funny memes and posts, so she had sent her a friend request. She felt drawn to her in some way. The woman had accepted immediately.

The message from her simply said, "Would you like to be my pen pal?"

Chapter 3 – The Connection

The replies Emily got back were varied. One woman said a flat-out no and then blocked her. Another woman was a hesitant no.

"Well. I don't know you. This could be a scam. I will not give my address to you. It is not safe." Emily could understand this and didn't push the issue.

But the third response via Messenger was what she was hoping for. "Sure," Rishat said. "But I don't write much."

"If it's too much time, I understand. I can see you are busy."

Emily replied after going back to look at Rishat's profile. She could see Rishat was married with a grown daughter and was active with the school children.

"Let's begin by chatting and emailing," she said.

Emily explained, "That's nice too, but I'm trying to see if the written word creates a more intimate conversation and relationship. Just evaluating some ideas."

"I'm sorry to say no then, but I tend to type and haven't used a pen in ages except to sign. And I have bad handwriting. Please understand." Her response was so genuine Emily was touched and felt an immediate connection.

"Absolutely! We can type if you like. I would love to know you better."

Emily sent her email address, and Rishat sent hers back with a thumbs-up.

Being extremely excited about this new adventure, Emily sent out an email right away telling Rishat some things about herself that she believed were more intimate than the superficial posts on Facebook or social media.

It went like this:

Hello Rishat,

I am sitting on my patio this nice evening. The sky is blue, and the humidity is low. The neighborhood is quiet, except for the occasional motorcycle going by.

I hate the motorcycles. They are annoying in many ways but mostly because I lost my childhood best friend a few years ago in a motorcycle accident. So, the sound of them makes me cringe.

I visit my friend's grave occasionally and think about the memories of growing up together, sharing stories of first dates to first kisses. to being maid of honor in her wedding. It saddens me that I will not be able to grow old with her.

I don't talk about this to anyone, so I thought, 'This is what a confidante is for.' These are the kinds of things we don't talk about on social media. The personal things to share.

I have not had a best friend in a long time. Someone to share the little thoughts and everyday things going on in life, like what I'm having for dinner or what we should watch on TV tonight.

I talk to Spot a lot. Spot is my cat, as you can see from all the pictures on my Facebook page. She is quite spoiled as cats go, but she is my true companion these days.

I am a Child Psychologist and Family Counselor at the County Mental Health Hospital in town. I love my job and the kids I work with.

I taught at a preschool, working my way through college before getting hired here. I saw on your profile that you teach. Something we have in common.

My mother died a few years ago. A serious car accident that my father died in brought on early dementia, and eventually, I had to put her in a home. We talked every day and spent most weekends together while she was sick.

I went to visit as much as I could. But after a while,

she didn't recognize me, and I had to stop visiting because she would get so agitated, not knowing who I was anymore. It was a blessing when she died, knowing she didn't have to live like that, in that place anymore.

I will have my coworker's dog in a couple of weeks while he and his girlfriend go to Hawaii. She is a miniature pincher and incredibly old. She cannot hear, and her eyesight is about half functional. On top of that, she is overly attached to Kurt. So, she sits and waits for him to come home.

She stares at the door when we are in the house or wanders around the yard when we are outside, looking for him. It's so funny but kind of sad. The last time I had her, she got loose and took off down the road like she was going home. (I want my daddy) lol.

She and Spot get along, though. Or I should say Spot lets her stay here and doesn't give her a tough time about it.

I love your idea of handmade bookmarks for the kids you tutor who are going off to university, especially the ones you posted on Facebook. That is so personal and lovely.

I am planning a vacation to the National Parks of America in September. I am so excited; I have started packing already. Lol Just the small stuff, but my suitcase is getting fuller and heavier, so I may have to adjust it before I go. It's hard to pack for twelve days and half hot, half chilly weather.

I find myself fascinated with covered bridges, and I take trips to see them around Pennsylvania, taking pictures in all seasons. I have them printed and covering my wall in frames.

Once, I pulled into a field to get a better view of a bridge, and when I got out of the car, a flock of butterflies came up to swarm around me. What an exceptional experience. I found it to be more spiritually fulfilling than church.

The church bells across the street ring, and it is 8: 00. It is time to go in. The air is getting chilly, and I must catch the episode of 'Young Sheldon' I missed the first time. They are showing a rerun of it tonight. Young Sheldon is one of my favorite shows.

Looking forward to hearing from you.

Emily (Em for short)

In the subject line, she put – Special stuff between friends.

The next day at work, Emily was in the lounge on her break when Kurt came in to eat.

"I do not want or expect an answer right away. Part of this process is the delay. If we were writing letters,

I would mail it and wait for a reply." She told him as they ate about having a pen pal from India.

He was skeptical.

"So, you are writing to someone in India you have never met?" he said. "Did you give him your home address?"

"No!" Emily replied. "First of all, he is she. Second, she is a friend on Facebook, and we connected via Messenger. Then, we exchanged email addresses. So, no, I did not give her my home address. Besides, she is married and has a child."

"She could still be he and defrauding you. People make up profiles all the time, even making up husbands and kids."

He tried to sound concerned, but Kurt had known Emily for a long time, and she was strong. She would not let herself be taken in by someone like that.

"I am being safe, I assure you."

But Emily had to admit to herself she was a little nervous. She had looked at Rishat's profile and searched her other social media sites, concluding that this was a legitimate person and someone safe to talk to.

Rishat even had a blog set up that anyone could access. Her profile had been established for years, and she had many friends and family. She did not post many pictures of them on Facebook but claimed her privacy, which was acceptable and practiced by many.

It's a healthy boundary. Nothing creepy about that!

She did not hear back from Rishat after she waited for a couple of weeks, so she sent another email, talking more about herself and being anxious to get to know Rishat personally. Her second letter said:

Hi Rishat,

Just got in from work. It was a day of catching up on paperwork, the part of my job I don't care for much. I'd rather spend time with the kids. Now I am waiting for some mac n cheese microwaving for dinner.

Nothing is going on tonight with any of my groups. The rain is keeping everyone in.

As you have seen, I am a co-organizer for a women's group and a hiking group. The women's group schedules activities throughout the month, such as lunches, dinners, movies, game nights, concerts, etc. Every member is an organizer, so anyone can schedule an event for others to attend.

As a leader in the hiking group, I look for parks and trails closer to the area I live in, east of Pittsburgh.

The other leaders (there are three of us) schedule hikes in and around Pittsburgh. It works out well for those who don't want to travel too far to get to a hike. We may pack lunch or snacks or go somewhere to eat after the hike.

Being a part of big groups like this is rewarding, and it is entertaining meeting new people all the time, but it is usually different people turning out, and once again, that connection is missing, that one-on-one personal touch. Even the conversations get repetitive and dry. The hope of meeting a close friend or life partner is waning.

I'm just as happy to spend time alone, reading, putting a puzzle together, or watching TV. Actually, I love to color in coloring books. It sounds childish, but it is so relaxing for me. I am not much of an artist at drawing or painting my own pictures, though I try, but I can create a colorful masterpiece for a coloring book page. (smiley face) BTW: My coworker thinks you may be scamming me. I told him you are harmless. lol

Well, I'm off to eat my dinner and read for a while before bed. Oh, I also belong to a book club. I saw that you like to read and wondered if you would recommend books on philosophy that I might enjoy reading.

Take care. Hope to hear from you soon.

She paid more attention to Rishat's social media activity but tried not to be creepy about it. She also began researching the traditions and culture of India to better acquaint herself with Rishat's background and way of life and to share conversations with her.

It was fascinating to learn all this new information about her faith and religion. Emily hoped Rishat would talk about her beliefs and that they could share their faith journey together.

She noticed Rishat liked her Facebook posts all the time and she was happy to see her on there, but this was the type of thing that Emily felt was lacking substance. She didn't want to push her and make her uncomfortable. A friendship had to develop naturally or not at all.

After a month, Emily began to think she was not going to hear from her after all. Perhaps she had second thoughts about confiding personal details of her life with a stranger halfway around the world.

"It would be understandable. There are too many terrible things going on in the world," she said to Spot one evening while the cat stared up at her, eating alone at the dinner table.

She was about to give up on the idea when she received a note from Rishat through Facebook

Messenger.

"Just a quick message to say I've enjoyed both your emails. Will be replying to both this weekend with every little thing that's been keeping me too busy to write. Meantime, I'm here, girlfriend, for a chat whenever you need to share little things like the AC isn't working, it's too hot to fall asleep, or you're afraid you've spoiled your cat."

She inserted a smiley face, and Emily felt very warm inside.

Chapter 4 – The Bond

Rishat had to laugh at the thought of being a scammer. But this had concerned her too and was the reason for the long delay in writing back. She waited and watched to see if Emily would show any sign of being a little off or just a scammer herself.

We cannot be too careful these days, she thought, as she was making some coffee to start her day. This day would not be a busy one, and some housekeeping would require her attention.

As she sat at the table sipping her coffee, she read Emily's letters again. She checked out her Facebook page and looked at the pictures she posted of her many activities. She wondered why Emily would be lonely. She seemed to have so many friends and activities in which she was involved. But then Rishat felt a bond with her. After all, she felt lonely, with all these people around her, and had no real feelings of closeness. She had her husband, of course, for many years, but the relationship between them had become routine and dry, with no intimacy.

Thinking of all this, she wrote:

Dear Em, your name is as cute as you are in your pictures.

I must first say I am laughing hysterically at the thought of being a scammer, but then I have not told my husband and daughter about you, for that very thing is what they would think of.

I do understand the excitement you feel about your upcoming trip. I had one planned, too, last year. It was with my daughter, and we went to visit Kolkata (city in West Bengal) and Assam (state), both in eastern India, so quite across from where we are living in the west coast.

I was partly looking forward to it and partly dreading it for different reasons. (She remembered confiding this in Kumar, but he was indifferent to her. A girlfriend might understand better.)

In Kolkata, I visited old school and university friends whom I hadn't seen for ages. We were students when last together! We've kept in touch sporadically, but I didn't know quite what to expect. I know I have changed a lot! But it turned out to be great fun!

The festival of 'Durga Puja' is in October, and I wish to show my daughter, Jaya, the grand spectacle of this festival in Bengal and Assam. And in Assam, it was going to be meeting relatives, my parents' relatives. My parents passed away in 2014 and 2016, and their siblings and cousins are mostly gone too, but cousins, nieces, and nephews, even a few grand nieces and nephews, still live in Assam. I hadn't met them since 2015. So, we met as many as possible in a brief time.

It was also our first mother-and-daughter solo trip. My husband had school and could not make it. The fact is, I was not sure I wished to reconnect with my roots. They're nice and have been urging us to come so we can spend time together and reconnect.

It was for my daughter that I went, who wished to meet her extended family, and she also thought it would be good for us to reconnect with friends and family on my side. The last few years have been focused on my husband's family.

I've lived such a "pendulum life" for the last 20 years (since coming to Ahmedabad in 2003). After an arranged marriage and having a child - swinging solely between home and work - I tutor students at home to prepare to attend university - and I seem to have lost quite a bit of social confidence. It's a 5-9 kind of job where if I'm not at lessons, I'm preparing and planning for it at home!

We have, of course, taken holidays in between work time, but my husband dealt with all the details. I kind of just went along. So, I worried about having to deal with travel and hotel details. Not overtly, because my daughter is smart with things, but I'm afraid of not pulling my weight. Silly of me, really!

I'm so impressed by your ability to plan, organize, and follow through on travel! My husband and I plan to visit game reserves and sanctuaries in India when his schedule allows.

His father passed away last October, and so his mother, in her seventies, 'needs' quite a bit of attention. She isn't used to being alone and spent three months with us recently, which was difficult for me, as she expects to be waited on hand and foot.

I had to keep her feeling loved and cared for in her newly widowed state and, manage a household, and keep up with my students! So, his annual vacations are likely to be spent with her. He says we'll also be visiting places, but I'm skeptical.

Even when my father-in-law was alive, they were very demanding, and we had to spend most of our vacation time with them. You're getting the family dynamics here, I think!

There's a line you posted on Facebook about spouses coming to dislike time spent together. It's true to some extent. My husband and I used to discuss everything and talk nineteen to the dozen before we married.

But after Jaya was born, his highly demanding job and looking after the baby, we shared the parenting chores, to be fair, took its toll.

We went through the usual highs and lows and are dependable partners now who know each other's strengths and weaknesses and accept them. But we don't talk as much as we used to.

There are worries about school on his mind, and I'm bored with school worries! We're partners and stand by each other loyally, but in private, there's the occasional poking of each other's sore spots!

Now he has got me doing this consulting job at his school so I will be there with him. It will keep me busy.

Yet, I get what you mean about whether you will meet someone right for you. Emily, I'm fairly sure there's someone you'll meet on your travels or social events who wants a friend and partner just the same as you, and you'll team up to spend the rest of your days together. That's the story I'm rooting for.

You come across as a warmhearted and genuine person, and that is a rare find these days. I feel incredibly happy to be your friend.

There's somebody just waiting to enter your life and become a part of your inner circle. You're the kind of person who's needed in everyone's life.

But I hope you meet someone who appreciates and values you for who you are. At our age, it's more likely you will because expectations should be more realistic, tempered by experience.

I don't know if I'm right, but instead of waiting for one person to share all your moments with, maybe share the moment you're in with the nearest person right then if there's anyone.

However, there's always you – the inner you who knows you inside out and, therefore, loves you as you are. It may sound silly, but I enjoy my inner 'dialogues' with myself these days.

The problem I have with my daughter is that she is a good-hearted folk but doesn't see the need to compromise with her physical comfort. My daughter tells her father that he and I grew up with strict parents and limited means, so we were frugal when we were growing up.

But her parents have much more, so it's only reasonable that she should spend money more freely and live a more comfortable life than we did at her age.

This generation does not see the need for 'independence' by giving up on comfort. I don't try to argue. I tell Jaya that if she can earn enough to follow the same lifestyle, that'll be fine. But she shouldn't come to dislike herself if she can't.

Feeling happy now enjoying what we have is better than wasting time and energy on yearning after things out of reach.

I wouldn't recommend reading any book on a particular philosophy. When I read fiction, poetry, or any other topic of interest, I sometimes come across a line that makes me pause, and I carry those words in my head afterward till they imprint into my brain and shape my response to life. That's my kind of philosophy.

On the other hand, whenever I read the work of a specific philosopher, I find myself disagreeing with some part of it, and that distracts me from the parts I agree with and makes me suspect my own responses. Am I making sense?

It's like your moment with butterflies. Bridges seem to be real and symbolic in your life. You've suffered yet come safely across your negative experiences by building bridges over to the other side. I feel you as a resilient human being who has always made time to care for those in need, to reach out with love.

Emily - you don't need a church. You have love in you, as Jesus wished all humans to have. It is the churches of this world that need you. If you feel lonely at times, it is because you are yet to love yourself as much as you love those around you - I think?

But I'm getting all philosophical here, and my email

As Rishat reread her letter before sending it, she worried about offending Emily with her words. Her intentions were not mean but loving.

From the exchange they had so far, Emily seemed like a strong and confident young lady who could take hearing the truth. This was a quality she admired very much in her and anyone else.

She had raised her own daughter that way and Jaya had always been brutally honest with her as she grew up, but always respectfully.

Sometimes it hurt Rishat's feelings to hear the things Jaya would say about her – that she was not open or outgoing, that she was strict, that she was submissive to a fault.

When Jaya turned 18, Kumar wanted to arrange her marriage with a young man at his school who was a teacher and would be a good provider. Jaya was not interested in marriage and wanted to attend university to become a teacher herself. She did not want to sacrifice her dreams as her mother did.

Rishat admired her strength to stand up for what she wanted, unlike herself, giving up her own dreams to do what she was told by her parents and then her husband.

This was the way she was taught in her culture and religion. To go against it during that time would be difficult. They raised Jaya to be her own person, strong and independent.

Now, with this new friend (she would not tell her husband and daughter about her pen pal because she feared their disapproval and criticism), Rishat saw another country and way of living.

They do not always see or hear of the things that go on in the United States, nor is what they do always hear the truth.

Of course, on Facebook and social media, the world is open and shared as it is for all to see. The truth can no longer be hidden or de-emphasized.

The wars are a concern to all, and with the invasion of Ukraine by Russia, there is always worry about how far this will go.

Rishat often thought about taking Jaya to flee to America, but Jaya would not go. They are loyal to their country, India, and would not leave unless it became peril.

"Are we safe here?" she asked Kumar when the fighting started.

She was concerned about Jaya being away from home.

Veer Narmad South Gujarat University was not extremely far from home, but Jaya was happy with being far enough away from her parents to have privacy and enough independence. Rishat liked that, too.

"India has not taken any action to side with Ukraine and are taking advantage of the lower prices for gas and continue to purchase weapons from Russia. India will continue to maintain ties to both Russia and the West with a posture of strategic ambivalence," Kumar said. "They are resisting a U.S. push to directly oppose Moscow while calling for peace and cooperation on what common ground there is."

Kumar knew a lot about the political aspects of the country and nation, more than Rishat even wanted to.

She did not care to see or hear about news of this, nor did she want to participate in the conversations others were having at the neighborhood grocers while shopping since she preferred to shop from her friendly neighborhood grocer rather than ordering everything online.

She enjoyed exchanging nutrition tips and learning

from the old grocer how to select the freshest fruit.

But being out to interact with people meant hearing about these things she cared little for and never got pulled into the conversations.

That is where my strength is. Taking care of my home and family.

Chapter 5 – Pictures And Conversations

Rishat was meandering about the apartment, moving slowly this morning for some reason. She didn't really have much to keep her busy since it was just Kumar and her in this small apartment.

She bathed the dog and groomed him. She would go out later for some dinner items. Maybe she would try a new recipe from the cookbook Jaya had given her.

When she sat down to check her emails, she discovered the last one she had sent Emily didn't have the pictures attached. She had wanted to send them to put Em's mind at ease about being a stocker. (Still chuckling at the thought)

Emily was still awake at 1:30 am when her phone notified her that a message had come in. She could not imagine who would be sending her a message at this hour. Sitting up, she retrieved her phone, unlocked the screen, and swiped open the message.

It was from Rishat, and it said, "Although I attached three pics in my email reply to you, I think they are not visible. Can you see them, or should I send again?"

Emily replied, "Two of them came through, but I

cannot open the third. You and your husband make a nice couple. And your daughter is beautiful. Thanks for sharing. I noticed you don't post pictures on Facebook. Many people are private about that. I'm glad I got to see them."

"This was the third."

A picture came in of Rishat sitting with another woman. She did not say who the woman was, and Emily didn't want to pry.

"And this is my daughter on her Convocation Day at her school. She topped her department and was awarded a gold medal."

"She looks like you. I'm sure you are so proud. You are a wonderful mother."

"Yes. We were happy for her."

"I'm curious. What time is it there?" Emily suddenly realized it was the middle of the night here in the US.

"It is exactly 11:26 am. I've just finished bathing, wiping, and blow-drying the dog. Back aching." She attached a smiley face.

"It is 1:56 am here. Once again, I cannot sleep," Emily wrote.

"Oh, dear. I, too, have insomnia. It's so tiring. I didn't sleep last night. What do you do to fall asleep?" Rishat asked.

"I have been watching National Geographic documentaries on nature and animals in the wild, preparing for my National Park vacation. Some are incredibly good. Some are too gruesome. I just finished a bowl of honeycomb cereal. I'm hoping I'll fall asleep now my stomach isn't growling anymore." She inserted a smiley face.

"Oh. I love watching them too," Rishat said. "But I don't like to see any kills. I have a really silly insomnia remedy which works only if I'm calm enough. In the past whenever I've tried to meditate, I've found myself nodding off. So now I try to repeat a mantra and focus my mind, and usually I fall asleep."

"Meditation is good," Emily replied. "I have done that in the past. I've tried yoga too but am not able to balance well."

A picture came in of an old labrador. "This is Cujo, fourteen years old. He was my daughter's birthday present when he was under a month old. He was abandoned at the school, and Kumar thought he would make a good pet."

"Aw, I really would like to have a dog, but they are too much to take care of for me with a full-time job. And who would take care of it when I travel," Emily said.

"I had my own pet German spitz when I was in school. It survived seventeen years till Jaya was a toddler before he passed away. It was still heartbreaking. I never wanted another. This one just walked into my life.

"I'm shocked at pets being abandoned. Of all human cruelty, this is one of the worst. India is particularly bad, especially with people getting pets during the Covid lockdown and then abandoning them without a second thought!

"I've fostered wild birds (semi-grown) which were then released into the wild, and three baby squirrels and a Koel (Indian Cuckoo).

"But life with dogs in a small apartment is hard on the dogs. Luckily, mine have had the school grounds through the greater part of his day while I am there. And my husband has agreed to let him visit the campus if I don't stay with this consulting job permanently."

"I once found a duck that was injured and took him to a nature reserve," Emily told her story. "They sent me a letter a few months later telling me he had made a complete recovery and been released to the wild. What an exciting feeling that was."

"But you must try and sleep now – and I'll stop chattering. Good night and peaceful sleep to you." A heart emoji followed.

"Yes! I guess I should try to sleep now. I've so enjoyed our conversation. I will send an email when I get a chance. Good night."

Feeling peaceful, Emily rolled over and fell right off to sleep as soon as she signed out.

Rishat sat on the couch in her living room, drinking tea and pondering the friendship that was developing between them. It happened so quickly. They just came together so easily, as though they had known each other for a lifetime.

She felt a desire to write this to her, so she began her email,

Dear friend,

In your email when you talked about losing your best friend to death, I want to say I haven't lost any friend to death yet but there's another kind of loss when friends grow apart in their busy lives and a coldness seeps in. It hurts but sharing our lives can't be forced.

I wasn't much aware of it when I myself was extremely engrossed in work and home, but I feel it now. We have WhatsApp groups, but rarely do we say much except greet each other on birthdays or special occasions.

Once she sent this letter, Rishat decided to take Cujo for a walk to River Front Park on the Sabarmati River, not too far from their apartment.

It would do her some good to be out and Cujo too. The temperature was cool but comfortable on the water.

She went past the play area, where she took Jaya many times when she was young.

As she walked, she was reminded of their youth and the fun times with Kumar and Jaya, picnics and just playing on the beach, making sandcastles with tunnels that went all the way through. You could feel each other's fingers in the middle.

She laughed when she thought of the times together and missed them very much.

When she and Cujo finally got tired of walking, she

got him back in the car.

She knew of a place nearby where they sold specialty men's clothing.

She decided to shop for a shirt for Kumar that maybe he would like. It would be a gift with the special dinner she would make for no reason tonight, attempting to rekindle the romance between them.

Cujo lay quietly on the back seat, sound asleep, so she also ran in quickly at a grocery store she passed on the way home; she got the items she needed for dinner and headed home to start preparing for Kumar to come home.

When he arrived, his new shirt was wrapped up in paper, setting on the table for him to open.

"What's this?" he asked as he sat down for dinner.

"A new shirt for work," Rishat said.

"I have so many shirts, Rishat."

He put it aside and welcomed the dinner she set in front of him.

"I saw it in a store window and thought you might like it."

"Well, thank you, but we should not spend money on things we don't need," he said in an agitated voice.

They ate in silence, and when he finished, he went to

his office to work. She sat at the table alone.

Her life felt kind of empty, but it was what she had, and she chose to make it the most she could.

Though she understood their money situation was tight now with Jaya at university and the costs to keep her, she still felt hurt that he did not appreciate her effort to do something special for him.

She cleaned up the kitchen and went to bed early with her book.

Chapter 6 – Long Distance Talks

Once they got started, the emails got longer, and the messenger conversations came more often, sometimes in the middle of the night for Emily and sometimes in the middle of the night for Rishat, but eventually they found that morning and evening plateau fit for both of them.

Emily began to be excited about going home to read or chat online with Rishat. During her hours at work, she enjoyed the time she spent with the kids and families, giving guidance where needed, but these interactions sometimes made her acutely aware she did not have a family of her own.

The problems some of these families faced were extreme and Emily always thought she never wanted to have that. What if all those problems happened to her? She shared that in an email with Rishat that night.

"I don't know what I'm missing out on." She started her letter saying.

I see so many families at work having problems and think that could be me. I don't know if I'd have what it takes to be a good mother.

My parents were not bad parents by these measures.

They weren't always warm or affectionate, but they did the best they could, and I'm not so bad off as some of the kids I see come through here.

I don't even talk to my brother because after my dad died, he wanted nothing to do with taking care of our sick mother.

Do you still arrange marriages in India? Is that easier or more successful?

Does your work with the kids you tutor affect you like that? Do you think you'll ever get a job doing the work you do now and don't get paid for?

You should, you know. What you are doing now, is that a sort of volunteer work? Is there such a thing as that there?

Now I'm rattling on. Good night. (sleepy smiley)

Em

"Doesn't your constant curiosity about Rishat's culture offend her?" Kurt asked one day at lunch.

"If it does, she isn't saying anything," Emily answered.

She wondered if her questions were making Rishat uncomfortable, but she believed they were not. She seemed to enjoy talking about herself and some of her thoughts and ideas. Saturday, Rishat sent Emily a message saying she was sorry she hadn't written yet and would write as soon as she could.

Emily responded, saying, "No pressure. Only write when you have time."

She had replied, "I know, but I want to write. I like writing to you. Didn't you begin the pen pal project to explore writing relationships across distance? You'll be interested to know that I haven't written in my diary since I began writing to you."

And then: "First thing Sunday morning, I've emailed you, and I feel good doing so."

Rishat's reply said:

My dear Em,

You are overthinking this all. I think you would make a wonderful mother someday. You are doing well with your job. You're such a supportive person. You would probably be the family glue in your generation and the next.

Some people are born helpers, just as others need help. It's nature's way of safeguarding our species. And it is an instinct to reach out to the most trustworthy person. It sounds like that is you for so many people. About my jobs here, some schools in metro cities do have a few volunteer parents who come in to help on specific occasions.

I know a school where they help out as escorts for small children on the school bus. Or else, qualified parents may come in for a workshop with students on dental hygiene, cyber safety, diet, mental health, etc. etc.

This is what I feel is fair. The reason for this is, private schools charge good fees and can afford to pay part time workers the minimum wages as per labor laws. Government schools are subsidized but have strict nonvoluntary rules.

India has many qualified yet unemployed people who wish to teach but don't find a vacancy.

Yet there are government schools, especially in rural and remote areas, with absentee teachers and practically no teaching infrastructure or other resources and facilities.

Here, NGOs (non-governmental organizations) with volunteers who donate time and effort to step in and instruct the local children.

So, the scenario has shifted totally from the US setup of neighborhood community schools, where students can walk or cycle to school and parents can volunteer their spare time as a kind of community service. And that is what I do now.

Here in India, yes, they still do arrange marriage, but usually with full involvement of the prospective bride/groom. The level of cooperation depends on the family dynamics of each specific case.

The apple usually doesn't fall too far from the tree. Sometimes, instead of relying on chance to meet the right partner, young men/women prefer to specify their preferences (demands?!) and leave it to the marriage bureau (apps, these days?) to find the best match.

But of course, in some instances, despite age-appearance-profession paycheck & perquisite, location, etc. matching as specified, there are clashes when expectations are too high on either side.

There is a lot of divorce and separation. And more young people with good incomes prefer not to marry but to enjoy themselves with friends, partners and with no lasting commitment.

There is a plan for your life, Em, and you will find it when you are ready.

Now I have gone on for a bit, rattling as you say, and I need to start my day.

Much love to you, Rishat

Emily got this letter Saturday night and could not sleep. She got on Messenger and reached out to Rishat.

"I just received your email. Thank you for all the kind things you said to me. I often wonder how people see me and there you are, far across the world, seeing in me many qualities just from letters and messages and social media."

Rishat replied immediately, "Hello. You are awake. You can tell a lot from a person on social media, but of course, you may find the person not always is genuine with what they post. Your posts and memes are always about doing good, and you seem to have that quality about you in your letters also."

Emily said, "I am awake. And how about you? What are you doing today?"

"I find that I have nothing to do. I am enjoying some of 'me' time, and Cujo is wanting to go for a walk. I may do that in a while. We will go to the park on the river and walk along the paved walkway along the water. It is one of my favorite places to be."

"I love the water too. I have always dreamed of owning a lake house like the one in the movie called *On Golden Pond*. Have you ever seen that?"

"I have not seen it," Rishat said. "I do not watch much Television. I like to read, and right now, I am reading Revolutionaries: The Other Story of How

India Won Its Freedom. I got several books from my daughter that require my attention, too."

Emily replied, "It is an endearing movie about two elderly people who have a cabin on the lake. They end up taking care of a twelve-year-old boy for their daughter. It's so good. I hope you get a chance to see it.

"But I know what you mean about reading. I belong to two book clubs, and it is hard to keep up with sometimes. Well, my dear, I am sleepy now and should get to bed. Enjoy your day."

"Sleep well, Em!"

Chapter 7 – Emily

It is coming up on Passover and Easter when Emily is most involved in church activities. The bible study and faith-sharing group meet every Wednesday night during Lent.

Emily was not leading a group this year and decided not to attend either. The struggle was not with her faith so much as with the structure of religion itself. *All the rules!*

She just didn't know if she believed all this dogma and tradition. And the hypocrisy in the church was enough to push anyone away if you didn't understand it all clearly and keep it in perspective.

Emily thought, *I believe in God. I do believe in the birth, crucifixion, and resurrection of Jesus. But the rest of it…*

She thought about Rishat and wondered about her religious beliefs. She decided to get some books about Hinduism and study some of it.

As she did, she learned the culture was quite different and not what she would accept as her own faith.

At work, she broached the subject with Kurt.

"I want to ask Rishat about her stand on religion but

didn't want to risk offending her. I'll have to be tactful."

"That is a touchy subject, religion. Good luck with that." He was of no help. "By the way, I'm dropping the dog off Friday evening around 6ish. Is that okay?"

"Sure. I'll be home doing nothing." She said in a distained voice.

"You sound bitter. Are you getting bitter?" He asked.

"No!" Emily tried not to sound surprised he had asked that, though she was. "I don't think I'm bitter."

Kurt laughed and walked out, taking his soda and half-finished sandwich to toss in the garbage at the door.

And now I am eating alone again.

After lunch was her session with the Cosby couple. It was hard to get through. They were not going to make it, and she knew it.

He was obviously having an affair, and she was completely indifferent about it. But Emily had to go through the motions.

"So, did you do the communication exercises I gave you to do before you came in today?"

"No!" they both said in unison.

"Okay. So would you like to work on them now?"

"No!" again, in unison.

"What are we doing here? Do you want to continue to work on this marriage, or are we over it, cause frankly you're wasting my time and your money."

Emily was not holding back now. They needed to make a choice, and she knew she had to push them to it, or they'd drag this out forever.

"What about the kids?" Jenna Cosby asked.

"Look. I know divorce is really hard on families and kids, and it's not something I would normally recommend. But neither of you are working on this marriage, and it feels to me like it's over.

It's your choice. If you manage yourselves maturely and make responsible decisions, the process can at least be less painful for everyone. The most important thing to remember is to stay open to communicating about issues such as custody, visitation, support, make this all as reasonably amicable as possible."

"She's going to take all my money," said Ted Cosby.

"I should take it all. You get to move in with that bimbo now and what do I have. Kids to feed and care for."

"See, that's the kind of communication that is going to drag you and the kids down a lot. Try to look at it in a more positive way. You all deserve to be happy, and you are not accomplishing that together. So how can we reach an agreement that will make everyone at least comfortable and not feeling like they are getting screwed over?"

"I don't know." Ted said. "I know I'll have to pay support for the kids and that's fair, but you need to go back to work too and help out. You don't love me anymore. Let's move on."
Jenna began to cry. "It's just going to take me some time."
"It will take you all a lot of time to heal from this, but the best thing is to not make it harder for each other or the kids. Cause that's even worse to get over in the long run," Emily said. "I can continue to see you individually for as long as you need to come."

They left, and Emily felt a sense of sadness for them. The journey ahead was going to be long and hard. At home, she crawled into bed and began to write to Rishat.

Hey kiddo,

I had the worst day, and I'm feeling like I need a friend. A couple I have in therapy are just not making it, and today, they decided they would call it quits.

I know it's for the best, but I feel like I failed this family. The kids mostly. Logically, my brain knows I had no control over it; my heart just hurts for them.

So, I came home, put my jamas on, and crawled in bed with a bowl of honeycomb. Needing a little take care of me time. A nice part of being single!

We are busy here preparing for Passover and Easter. Being Catholic is difficult for me sometimes. Born and raised, they call us cradle Catholics.

It is just a way of life and not really a complete acceptance for me. I have lots of questions, and they don't like that very much. They don't want you challenging their beliefs.

So, this year I've kind of backed out of the traditional happenings like bible studies and such. I'm doing my own reflections, reading meditations, and journaling.

What is this time like for you? Do you practice any religion personally?

Being single carries a stigma too about morality that we contend with here. Is it like that there?

I'm feeling very sleepy now. Hope to hear from you soon. Love, Emily. Sleep came fast and easy.

Chapter 8 – Rishat

Dear Em,

First, it has been a long time since I am referred to as 'kid.' (heart emoji)

I'm sorry not to have written for so long!

Now, where do I begin? Well, my daughter came home for a break, and when she's here, all my free time seems to be spent with her.

And I haven't had much free time, because I'm trying to read several interesting books together, like I used to do, "Once upon a time, long, long ago!"

But I think I've lost that focus of my youth, or maybe there's much more stuff demanding my attention more frequently now!

My daughter's given me two books, one a murder mystery by Donna Tartt and another, an award-winning history non-fiction, Courting India, by Nandini Das.

Then, I was already on Stanislas. Dehaene's Brain and Consciousness, and another ancient text on Indian Philosophy, Ashtavakra Samhita - that's the Sanskrit title, but I'm reading an English translation of it alongside following some scholarly commentaries on the text and also a series of explanatory audio lectures. I'm also making it a point to regularly listen to some classical music and to audio lectures on art to quell the "philistine" in me!

Before you think I'm becoming all high culture and intellect - I'm also full of aches and pains! My neck and shoulders, my lower back and hips and my knees - these have been problematic for years, and the pain flares up from time to time, and it's that time again now!

I'm trying to follow through on physiotherapy exercise, applying heat and ointment and when that doesn't suffice, anti-inflammatory tablets - as prescribed by my orthopedist. But even my regular walking schedule gets interrupted or is followed by acute pain. I'm worried I may end up a cripple and a burden!

So, I don't give up and sit back, except for some brief spurts of self-pity. I'm trying my best to keep up regularly with strengthening exercises and walking.

So, with all of this going on, there's been little "mood" or time to write, of late.

I know you feel badly about the family situation, and you seem to have a good sense of 'it's not your fault.' You did the right thing to take care of yourself the way you did.

About singles ...hmmm! Honestly? I think most of them are the dearest, most unselfish, genuine, and spontaneous people I've ever met. They've maintained their identity without compromising on life to adjust with others.

There are the usual exceptions, and not everyone is at their best every day. But I think there's no problem with being single unless the person herself/himself feels lonely. Also, if s/he's unwell, aged, and feeble, etc. then some company/help becomes necessary. In our culture, aloneness is different from loneliness.

I've always said to my younger friends and students that I don't believe that happiness comes from being with others – friend, partner, spouse, child, whoever.

Happiness is within our own mental framework; we have to consciously choose to be happy with what we have. I used to grumble a lot about that in my life, that the only good is that nothing bad is happening.

Then, I realized that nothing bad happening is the best definition of happiness!

So, being single, one can still be happy, just as one can be happy after leaving a bad marriage or by not getting together with the wrong partner. Am I making sense here? But of course, your most authentic answer will come from a single person. I'm solitary with my books at home for the greater part of everyday now, and I've never been happier!

Love you, pen pal. Stay healthy and happy. Let's enter 2024 with our friendship becoming stronger. .

Rishat.

She honestly believed this as she said it to Emily, that being alone is the happiest now. Jaya is off to university; Kumar is spending more time at this job or on his trips home to take care of his family.

But she had dodged the question of religion and faith because she did not know how to answer. She felt the struggle a private matter and did not want to share her personal thoughts about it yet. She will tell her that next time.

That day, she left early to do her workshop at the school, taking Cujo with her to walk after her session with the students.

When she arrived, she set up her lesson on the board and went to see if there were any extra drinks in the lounge refrigerator before the students arrived.

Her throat felt dry, and she wanted water to drink during her presentation. There were no bottles, but some cups available for her to fill up from the faucet.

Back in the room, the students were coming in.

"Hello, Mrs. Navin," they all exclaimed when they

arrived and sat at the tables.

"Hello!" She greeted them each by name enthusiastically.

She was extremely excited to be there, and it would always show in her demeanor and presentation. She genuinely enjoyed the kids and loved teaching them. It also helped her forget her pain.

While most qualified parents may come in for a workshop with students on dental hygiene, cyber safety, diet, mental health, etc. Rishat always wanted to do something fun as well as learning, so her workshops always focused on reading or art of some kind.

"Today, I want talk about the importance of planting trees," she began. "If we can't stop the felling, we should at least plant to replace what we take."

One student asked, "Can we plan a day to go out and plant a tree?"

"I will look into that," Rishat exclaimed, loving the idea. "If we can't plant a tree, I'll at least put together a day of planting flowers in a pot as soon as the weather permits."

They were just as happy with that. They had some discussion time about planting and growing new life before it was time for Rishat to leave.

Cujo, who had sat in the corner very quietly awaiting his turn for her attention, jumped up as Rishat approached him.

"It's your turn, boy," she said and took him by the leash, leading him out to the walkway.

They went around the school and through the parking lot to the car, which was plenty all Cujo could do any more. It was all he could do to jump into the back seat of the car, panting heavily before falling asleep.

At home, Rishat got the dog settled in with food and water and then started dinner. She was making pakora, a savory deep-fried dish made with eggplant dipped in chickpea flour, seasoned with turmeric, salt, and chili spice, then deep-fried in ghee.

Another one of her favorite dishes, she has been treating herself a lot lately to foods she loves, perhaps comfort eating.

She was feeling exceptionally good about her life and thought about her new friend in the United States.

It is so nice to have a confidant. She thought about sending her a message to chat. *She is probably sleeping now.*

She was surprised to see Kumar in the door early before she was finished with dinner.

"Would you like some Assam tea?" she asked him.

Assam tea is a strong black tea grown in the Assam region that was one of their favorite drinks while relaxing to talk.

"Yes," he sat down at the table and sipped the tea while Rishat finished dinner. He talked of his day and what was happening with his parents, the same conversations they always had. She listened intently as a good wife should but secretly wished he'd ask about her day. He did not.

Once they sat together with their meal in front of them, they ate silently. After dinner, he would sit and read the news on his computer while she cleaned up the kitchen and did the dishes alone.

She thought about Emily and their conversation about being single. *Being married doesn't mean being happy. And it doesn't mean you won't feel alone.*

Chapter 9 – Kurt

At forty years old, I am still single!

It was Thursday night, and he was packing for his trip to Hawaii with Susan Blakely. He had met Susan at a speed dating event two years ago in Pittsburgh. They hit it off right away and went for drinks after, spending half the night talking.

In Kurt's eyes, she was a blue-eyed, blond beauty, and he couldn't understand what she saw in him. Not that he had low self-esteem cause he did not. He just knew she was out of his league.

But she stuck around this long, so he intended to propose to her on the beach in Maui.

The ring is packed. Check.

He made a list and checked it twice. Was he crazy? They had never really talked about marriage. He had no idea what she was looking for.

Being a prominent psychologist with a master's in relationship counseling, one would think this is something he would have addressed prior to the ring purchase.

"Am I crazy?" he asked Emily Friday night when he dropped Martha off.

Martha, a miniature pincher, had stayed at Emily's many times since she and Kurt had been working together, probably seven years now, and Kurt would trust no one else with her.

Martha walked right in and took her place on the couch, much to the dismay of Spot, who had to move out of her way.

"So, the two of you have never talked about marriage, kids, a future, nothing?" Emily asked, making him a cup of coffee as they sat down at the dining room table for a chat.

"No! Never!"

"Isn't this your first trip together?" she asked.

"Yes."

"Yes! You're crazy!"

Emily always knew she could be brutally honest with Kurt and he with her as well. That's the kind of relationship they had.

"I plan to ask her some questions to build up to the proposal. Ya Know! I'll take her to dinner one night and ask her about the future, what she's thinking, how she feels about kids, and all that. I mean, we'll just have the conversation and if I like the answers I'm getting, I'll propose. If not, I won't."

"And you'll just return the ring?"

"Yes," Kurt burst out laughing, realizing how ludicrous it was.

Emily just smiled, "Look, you're in love, and love is blind. We both know that. We've both seen it all too often. Don't be stupid on this trip. Think with your brain, Kurt. You're a terrific guy. Don't think this is your last chance for love and marriage. You know what that kind of thinking leads to."

"But I'm forty years old. I don't want to have kids when I'm in my fifties. I have two years invested in this relationship. If it doesn't work out, I'm starting all over," his despair was coming through loud and clear.

Emily was worried he was going to do something stupid in Hawaii.

"I know how you feel. I'm in the same situation. But trust me, I've seen a lot of marriages end because of desperation. What are we always saying? A bad marriage is worse than no marriage at all."

"Right," he got up and hugged her. "Thanks for the coffee and the pep talk. I'm glad we are friends."

"Me too," Emily said. "Fly safe and, most important, land safe."

They laughed.

Kurt drove home and finished packing. Then he

called Susan.

"Hi. You all packed and ready?"

"Yes, I am. I'm packing light. Just my new bikini," she said flirtatiously.

"Yummy!" he said. "Can't wait to see that. So, I'll pick you up about 6:30 am. That will give us plenty of time to get through security. We can have coffee or breakfast while we are waiting to board the plane."

"That sounds good. See you tomorrow."

On Saturday morning, Kurt and Susan boarded a plane to Hawaii. Kurt had the window seat. Susan sat in the middle, terrified of heights, with a sleep mask on and earbuds in, trying not to freak out.

"Why didn't you tell me you had a fear of heights?" he'd asked her when they boarded, and she began to freak out.

"I didn't think it was such a big deal," she replied.

"We're thousands of miles in the air! That's not a big deal?"

"Well, but we're enclosed in a plane," she was beginning to cry.

"It's fine! Just put your mask on and go to sleep."

Good thing he booked a straight flight with no layover. He was hoping they didn't get stuck in

Hawaii because she wouldn't get on a plane to come home. He'd have to buy a boat.

Fortunately, Susan had taken a tranquilizer and slept the entire way, rousing only once to get a drink and go to the bathroom, which Kurt had to walk her to.

Napili Sunset Beachfront Resort welcomed them with a Mai tai at the door, and the stress of the flight was forgotten. They settled into their room and made their way to the beach.

Jet lag prevented them from really enjoying the first day as they lay on the sand in the sun. The view was beautiful. They made sure to cake on lotion *cause sunburn isn't going to ruin our vacation!*

On the second day, they both felt more like human beings, able to explore the island and enjoy the tourist experience.

The first visit was to the aquarium in Makawao, where they saw the largest living tropical reef in the Western Hemisphere and an amazing immersive humpback whale experience.

Kurt really enjoyed this, but Susan didn't seem as interested.

"Where would you like to go next," he asked her, hoping to get a better response if she picked something she really liked.

"Back to the hotel," she said. "It's too hot out, and I just want to lay by the pool bar."

"But we came all this way, and I really want to see the sights. Let's do something inside with air conditioning. How about the Hawaii Mission House? It's a historic museum?" he asked.

She kind of moaned and said, "okaaay!"

He ignored her drama, and they caught the next bus to the museum. Kurt was disappointed they could not get onto a tour because it booked up so far in advance but still relished the displays and learning about the place.

"Look!" he said. "It served as an important force in Hawaiian politics, religion, economics, and social customs from 1820 to 1860. It's a national landmark! It's dedicated to preserving the history of Christianity in early Hawaii. These artifacts, photographs, and memorabilia are from the 19th century. Doesn't this fascinate you?"

"Not really." She was bored. "Is there food anywhere?"

"So, I guess you don't want to stay for the lecture this afternoon?"

He didn't wait for an answer.

He was getting hungry, too, and the bus was due to

come by in about twenty minutes. They used the restrooms and went to the bus pickup point to wait.

They couldn't decide on a restaurant and ended up going straight back to the hotel.

Susan got into her bikini and grabbed her beach towel. "I'll get something to munch at the bar," she said.

"I think I'm going to stay in the room for a while and rest. The heat is making me tired."

"Okay!" she replied as she walked out the door.

Kurt lay down on the bed, staring up at the ceiling. He thought about Emily. He picked up the phone and dialed her office number. To his surprise, she picked up the phone.

"Hello, Emily speaking."

"I thought you'd be with a client," he replied.

"I am in the middle of paperwork on the Chester child custody case. And why are you calling me in the middle of the afternoon from Hawaii?"

"To check on my dog," he lied. He needed some sound advice, and she would give it to him straight.

"Really!" she was skeptical. "Well, Martha is fine. Missing daddy as usual, but she and spot manage to antagonize each other just enough to stay entertained.

Now, why are you really calling?"

He laughed. Then he spilled his guts about how difficult the trip had been.

"We haven't even had the talk yet. And I'm beginning to think it isn't necessary. I'm realizing I don't want a future with her. How did I miss all these warning signs all this time?"

"You were in love. Or maybe in lust. Who knows? But what's important is you found out in time to make a better decision now." She sympathized with him because she knew how he felt.

In her twenties, she stayed in a relationship for three years until they started talking prenup. That was the end of it. They couldn't agree on anything.

"It's a lot of time invested, but it's not your whole life. Think of these couples we counsel who are married twenty-five, thirty years or longer. And they have to start over, sometimes in their 60's."

"I know you're right. It's going to be hard getting through the next couple days knowing I'm going to break it off when we get home," he was dreading that moment already.

"Well, try to have fun. Go exploring on your own and do what you enjoy. It's okay to be single. You might be more comfortable without her."

Kurt knew she was right. He decided to go down and lie on the beach for the rest of today, but tomorrow, he was going to explore the island without Susan.

He met her at the bar, and they ordered some food and drinks. There was a luau that evening, and it was a lot of fun for them both. They made love that night; after all, she did look good in that bikini. And Emily was right. It was lust that kept him with her all that time.

They spent the rest of the vacation going their separate ways and doing their own thing. The flight was long because they both knew what was coming. At least she got on the plane without having an anxiety attack.

Driving home, Kurt broached the subject.

"So, what did you think of the trip?"

"Are you going to break up with me?" she went right for the jugular.

"Do you think that is the best thing for both of us?" he asked, hoping she'd realize it was just as much for her as for him. "By this trip, do you believe we have a future together?"

"A future! No. I just thought we were having fun and enjoying each other's company.

It became obvious at that moment she had never

intended to have a future with him. Wow! He didn't see it.

"I am starting to feel like I want to settle down and have a family. As I get older, I realize I can't be in dead-end relationships anymore. Does that make sense to you?"

"Yes," she simply said, and they were quiet the rest of the way to her house.

Chapter 10 – Emily

When Kurt picked up Martha, Emily gave him a big hug.

"Come in and have some sweat tea. I just made it fresh."

"Sure," Kurt said, feeling down in the dumps, partly from the jet lag, partly from the breakup.

Emily poured two glasses, and they sat out on the patio. It was cool but sunny for a spring Sunday afternoon.

"So, how'd the breakup go?"

"Actually, better than I thought," he replied. "She was very reasonable. The fact that we enjoyed nothing together on this trip showed us we had nothing in common. She said she was just looking for fun." He chuckled at that. "How was I so blind thinking it was more?"

"Because that's what you were in it for. She didn't give you a clue that it wasn't what she wanted too. If you never talked about it, how would you know"

"You are right. I guess I just didn't talk about it because I thought the longer it lasted, the more likely it would turn into more," he just realized that himself as he was sitting there talking it out.

"That happens to all of us."

"Thanks for the talk and being a friend," he had been saying that to her a lot lately. He finished his tea, stood, and hugged her again because he needed it.

She handed him Martha's box of toys, blankets, and other doggy treats.

"See you at work tomorrow," she called as he walked out.

Just then, a message came over the phone, causing it to vibrate. She picked it up and swiped it open.

Rishat was saying, "Hi. How are you? I am not sleeping well. I am sick and looking for sympathy."

"Oh no! What is wrong?" Emily replied.

"A cough, and now I am not holding food down due to coughing."

"Are you doing anything for it? Have you seen a doctor? You stay in bed and get well quickly!" Emily said, concerned.

"In India, we keep a single clove in the mouth, biting down on it slightly at times. The pungent juice released stops the throat irritation and reduces the bouts of coughing."

"Oh! That sounds like a wonderful remedy. Does it

help with the stomachache as well?" Em said.

Rishat explained, "We have another Tutka (herbal remedy). In half a cup of hot water, we put some crushed powdered ginger, honey, and holy basil leaves, crushed. A small sip of this when the throat itches works well. Also, another home remedy for stomach pain is to boil caraway/carom seeds for a while in water and strain out the liquid. 1 – 2 teaspoons diluted in half cup of water."

"I must try that when I am sick next time. It's good to have natural remedies instead of medications with all the additives that make things worse. Are you getting sleepy yet?" Emily asked.

"Yes, I am. You are good to comfort and calm me with just this little bit of chat. I think I can sleep now. I will write you more soon," Rishat finished and said good night.

Emily glanced out the window and saw the sun had given way to rain. It would be a dreary day, after all. Then she remembered it was Palm Sunday. She did not even think about it until this moment.

She also thought about the fact that Rishat had not talked about her religious beliefs in her last email. She would not push.

She hoped Rishat would feel better soon. Her heart wished she could be there to take care of her, make her the teas and remedies she talked of, while she got her rest. She wondered if her husband did those things for her.

Many husbands don't. She remembered reading an article about Indian couples who are struggling to balance tradition with a desire to change.

The article said Indian marriages represent love and don't often explore what happily ever after entails. Many of the issues the couples face, such as divorce and the search for sexual gratification, are still considered taboo topics.

Emily hoped Rishat's marriage was a good one and she was finding gratification with her partner now. She wasn't getting that impression, though. She hardly talked much about him, and there were no pictures of them on Facebook.

But she is very private.

She found herself thinking about bringing Rishat to America to visit or even stay here.

What would she think about that?

It was time to finish this puzzle and get it put away. She spent the afternoon listening to music while doing her puzzle. A song from the Bee Gee's came on – How Deep is Your Love? She thought of Rishat.

Before getting into bed that night, she checked her

emails in case a message came in about work the next day. She discovered an email from Rishat.

Dear Em,

Happy Easter coming up to you and all your extended family!

I hope you and Spot are well and happy into your whirlwind Easter plans. You and Spot will probably be spending some quality time together at home that day, I assume? You can rest and recoup from all your exertions then.

Em,

I have not discussed my religious feelings and beliefs with anyone for a long time. And I know I have been putting it off with you.

I struggle to know what I think and believe. I am on a journey to find something but am not sure of what it is yet.

Easter in India begins with Lent and culminates on Easter Sunday with Christians all over, especially in Mumbai, Goa, and the Northeastern states, make elaborate arrangements for the festivities. There are churches full of people saying special prayers and rituals.

We do not decorate eggs here, instead buying painted eggs at the festivals to give as gifts to the children. During the festival, people exchange gift items with each other. I have always enjoyed this ritual and event every year.

I hope you understand my reluctance to discuss the manor of my faith at this time, so I do not offend you. You mean so much to me.

And I wish to resolve it and be sure of what makes sense to me. I'm sure I will get there someday.

I am feeling better and thank you so much for taking good care of me, if only in thoughts and prayers. Enjoy your holiday!

Love Rishat.

Emily decided to take some time before replying to this email to let Rishat know how she, too, was struggling with beliefs and faith. She wanted Rishat to feel free to talk to her about anything without worry of offending her.

She had already spent time learning about the religion of India and thought it different, but she would never judge her for what she believed.

She felt remarkably close to Rishat and wanted this to continue to grow.

Chapter 11 – Rishat

When Rishat woke up, the first person she thought of was Emily. She rose, washed, and dressed, then sat on the couch, checking her email and messenger, looking for a word from her.

She had the weirdest sensation, like emotional love but warm and embracing all over. She wished she could hold and cuddle with Emily.

Rishat had not been held or cuddled for a long time. The most intimacy she got now was hugs from her daughter when she returned for a visit.

Even the kids at the school did not hug much like they used to. When they did approach her, she found herself squeezing tighter than should be for that extra warmth she wasn't getting anywhere else.

Now that Emily had awoken in her this desire to explore her faith and beliefs, she got out some old books to skim through and refresh her thoughts.

She picked Bhagavad Gita, a renowned jewel of India's spiritual wisdom. It's a conversation between Lord Krishna and his intimate disciple, Arjuna, that offers a definitive guide to the science of self-realization.

Rishat had read this before and loved it's 700 verses of Hindu scripture written in Sanskrit that is a part of the great Hindu epic Mahabharata.

She spent the afternoon emersed in the book until Cujo let her know he needed a walk.

"OK. OK. Have I been neglecting you? Poor thing." Putting on his leash, she led him to the outside, and he bolted for the nearest area of grass he could find, no longer able to hold himself.

"Poor thing. How long have you been uncomfortable," Rishat said, petting him and offering a treat when he finally finished.

The day was partly sunny, and a slightly warm breeze blew through the streets off the river. They walked about a mile before Cujo decided he didn't want to go any further and Rishat had to coax him back to the apartment.

Her thoughts were on her marriage. It was important to her, and she wanted to work on it but felt alone and unwanted. Kumar was a good man and provider, yet he showed no interest in her physically. They were much like friends living together.

And not even good friends. She had more intimate conversations with Emily, a woman who lived halfway around the world and she had never met.

She wondered what it would be like to meet Emily. Would they have the same connection in person as they had on email? Is it possible to be one and not the other?

I must get these thoughts out of my head and focus on taking care of my husband.

She pulled out a chicken roast for dinner and spiced it up with chili powder, ginger, cloves, and the usual salt and pepper, popping it in the oven and setting the timer for one hour. Kumar would be home by then. She thought she would get dressed up a little for him. Perhaps do something special with her hair, use some smelly oils, and dab a little blush on her cheeks. Maybe this would spark something in their encounter this evening.

She had herself prepared and dinner on the table when he came in.

"You look especially pretty this evening," he noticed right away as he sat down to eat. "And you smell very nice."

"Thank you," she said. "I hope you enjoy the chicken prepared this way." She poured them a glass of Lassi, a yogurt-based drink that originates in the Punjab region of India. It's a fresh and cooling drink made with yogurt and different kinds of fruits. Rishat knew it was Kumar's favorite.

As they ate, she asked, "How was your day?

"Nothing much new going on at the school. We had some maintenance difficulties this afternoon with a plumbing issue. The board is going to have to vote on some upgrades if they want to keep the place standing upright in the future. Otherwise, it will be falling down around us."

"I noticed that the last time I was there. When I walked Cujo around, I noticed some areas outside where the concrete is chipping away and crumbling."

She enjoyed that they could talk about something they both knew about.

"Yes! That is exactly what I was talking about at the meeting last week. Something must be done."

His attention turned to his meal then, but Rishat was not ready to give up. "I pulled out a favorite book today and read most of the afternoon." He did not respond.

"Bhagavad Gita. I am thinking about my spiritual journey and would like to revisit some of my old views."

"Good. Good," was his only reply.

And she turned back to her food, feeling defeated. When he finished eating, he retired to the living room to read the news, and she cleaned up alone.

She crawled into bed with her book, and when he came in, she put the book down and asked if he'd like to talk for a while.

"I'm very tired, Rishat. Was there something important on your mind?" He asked.

"No. It can wait."

She rolled over and turned her light off but could not sleep.

Important! How about our marriage? Is that important to you at all!

Her mind was spinning, and when she heard him snoring, she got up to see about reading on the couch for a while, but she couldn't concentrate. She pulled up her email and found a letter from Em. Her heart leaped in her chest.

My dearest Rishat,

I too have struggled with my faith and religious beliefs, so I know how you feel. It is hard to talk about and very private. Please know that I do not judge you in any way. We are all on this journey and only God knows what is at the end. When you are ready, I am here.

I had a thought the other day about coming to visit India some time, to meet you, see the culture and enjoy time away. What would you think about that?

My friend Kurt would be happy to take care of Spot since I take care of his dog for him. Lol

I had the most enjoyable weekend with my hiking group. We hiked in a place called Apollo on the Roaring Run trail. It runs along the Kiski River. Everything is in bloom, and it made me think of new love.

One of the leaders of this group, Nick, has a house on the river. He does these 'Soup Hikes' he calls them, about once a month. Everyone brings food, and after a five-mile hike, we eat around a bonfire on the bank of the river. It's quite enjoyable.

He also has a shed full of kayaks, and whoever wants to stay can kayak the river the next day. I go home to sleep and back up since it's only a 40-minute drive for me. I'd rather get a good night's sleep in my own bed.

This group is large, and they always get a lot of people to show up, sometimes 30 or 40. There's a ton of food. The only downside is the bonfire is too large to make smores. Lol

Work is going well. We are busy, which is not necessarily a good thing. Too many people are getting divorced. Too many broken kids, broken families. Kurt asked me if I am getting bitter. Am I? It is hard not to.

But I still believe in love, just not the fairytale kind. There's no such thing as Cinderella and her prince. A woman must make her own dreams come true. Then learn how to share them with a man.

Well, that's my philosophy for life tonight. Sweet dreams and much love to you.

Em.

Rishat loved this letter. She also loved Emily. And the thought of Emily coming to visit her was exciting and frightening at the same time.

The belief she had practiced all her life about love and marriage came rushing in on her. She didn't know if Emily was having these feelings, too, but she knew she wanted to find out.

Chapter 12 – Sammy

It was cold on the streets of Pittsburgh this evening. The shelters were full. He'd tried Light of Life Rescue and Hearts of the Homeless. There will be no food tonight. They had run out of that, too.

He would wait for the restaurants to close and hit the dumpsters. Sometimes you found some really good meat they threw away. Other times, they didn't have many leftovers to pitch out, maybe some French fries or chili in bags that were a few days old. Ya had to make sure you were near an accessible auto garage with an open bathroom when you ate that stuff.

Bundled up in the blanket they handed him when they turned him away, he sat on the wall at Point State Park overlooking the Monongahela River. He looked down at the cold, dark water and thought about jumping but knew it wasn't deep enough here. He'd have to go up to the bridge to make the impact he wanted to accomplish.

But fatigue had set in from hunger, and he didn't even have the energy to kill himself.

How'd I get here!

He thought about school and his hopes and dreams for the future. Then the accident happened, and Dad died. Mom got dementia not long after, and Emily put her in that home.

He went to visit once or twice but couldn't take it seeing her in there like that. And then she didn't even know who he was.

He bounced around after high school from friend to friend, girlfriend to girlfriend, looking for someone, anyone, to love him and take care of him.

God knows Emily didn't. She made her way in life on her own. Put herself through college, got a job, and made good money. She had no idea how much he looked up to his 'big sister.' How much he wanted to be like her.

But she saw him as a no-good bum, taking advantage of people, living off of others. That's not how he wanted to be. He was embarrassed and ashamed of himself that he could not make it on his own as she did.

And he couldn't ask her. They just weren't taught to talk to each other like that growing up. There was no love or affection between them.

During his teen years, his parents moved his bedroom to the basement to make a bigger living room/dining room area. He came home from school one day to find all of his things moved. No discussion. No explanation.

"Your room's in the basement now," was all they said.

And there he stayed, in his own world, isolated from everyone. If it weren't for dinner being at the same time every day, he would never have eaten.

He was fifteen when Emily turned eighteen and moved to college. They made her room into a sewing room for Mom.

So, Emily left without saying goodbye. He left at eighteen himself but went in a different direction. He only saw her again when Dad died.

She sold the house, and she took mom to live in a nursing home. She didn't even ask him where he would go or what he would do. That was that.

Now, he sat on the bank of a river, wrapped in a blanket given to him by a homeless shelter, waiting for a restaurant to close so he could raid the dumpster for food.

How did I get here?

He thought when he moved in with Cheryl things might be looking up. He got a job at the local garage fixing cars during the day, and at night, he took some classes in mechanics.

Maybe someday he will open his own garage. He'd be a business owner. He'd call Emily, and she'd be proud of him.

But Cheryl had taken up with some characters at the bar she worked in, and they got busted using and selling. He was fortunate he had not been involved and knew nothing about it. One of life's breaks for him, at least.

After that, the garage let him go.

"Why? But I need this job. Please!" he begged them to let him stay on.

"We don't want anyone who'd been affiliated with that girl and drugs and all that working here. It'll give our place of business a bad name. You know how rumors start."

He couldn't pay the rent on the one room they were living in, even if he'd kept the job at the garage, so he had to leave. Of course, he had to quit school, too.

And that's how I got here!

As far as Emily knew, he was living somewhere with someone and doing fine. He wanted it to stay that way. He sure didn't want her seeing him like this.

It was time to go hunt for some food and then find a place to bed down for the night. Usually, someone would have a fire going somewhere, and he'd sack out with them for the night.

Tomorrow's another day.

Chapter 13 – Kurts' Holiday

He scheduled his appointments sparsely this week with Easter coming. His family expects him to be with Susan on Sunday. He hadn't told them yet that they were no longer together. He didn't know why.

He knew Emily would be alone on the holiday and thought about asking her if she'd like to join him for dinner. His family would really like Emily, and they wouldn't rib him so badly about Susan and why he wasn't married yet.

Typical family dynamic when you're single. Especially when you're 40 and single!

Susan and Kurt had seen each other once since their return from Hawaii, just long enough to exchange belongings they kept at each other's houses. And, of course, to have sex one last time, which happened spontaneously, and they both recognized it as a mistake.

"You had sex with her?" Emily exclaimed in the lunchroom over egg salad sandwiches.

"It just happened," Kurt said.

"I can totally understand that." Emily was completely aware of what it was to bounce in and out of a relationship that needed to be over, just for the sex. "It's a powerful drive."

"And when there's no prospects of ever having sex again, it's even more powerful." He put his head down on the table, faking a baby crying. "You're so good-looking! You can have women if you want them."

Kurt was very handsome, at six feet, with sandy blond hair, soft brown eyes, and a gentle personality.

"But I don't want sex. I want love."

His last client on Wednesday afternoon was his favorite kid, an eight-year-old boy named Luke. Luke came to him from a broken home. His mom had full custody and brought him to appointments.

He had ADHD, and Kurt put him on medication because the schools could not control him. Neither could his mother. They put the mother with her own therapist to have a support system and help her learn to manage the behavior issues they were having. With a team of doctors and therapists, Luke was doing really well.

"He's a genius with a photographic memory," He had told the other members of the team during their strategy meeting.

"With the right guidance, he'll go far. Unfortunately, the mother is in a bad situation."

His mother's therapist was John Henderson, and he stepped in.

"She is very smart and driven. She wants what is best for the kid and is doing everything she can to get out of poverty, into a better home and neighborhood. I know she'll provide him with every opportunity once she overcomes this."

This afternoon, the boy came in with a bruised face. His mother was beside herself.

"He got into a fight in the neighborhood. This kid was so much bigger than him, but Luke wouldn't back down. I had to pull him off and into the house. The cops came." She was almost in tears.

"It sounds like you need to get out of there," Kurt said.

"I have some money coming in from income tax. I'll be using that to move. It can't come soon enough for me. But Luke, you need to stay out of trouble, please."

She pulled him in and hugged him tight.

"Ok. Let's go talk about this." He took Luke back to his office and spent the hour talking about keeping himself and his mom safe.

He always played a couple of games to bond and create a safe environment for the kids to open up.

When they left, Kurt was writing up his report and the phone rang.

"When are you coming home?" It was his mother calling about the holidays.

His family still lived in Rochester, NY, where he grew up, about a five-hour drive from Greensburg.

"I just finished my last client for the day. I'll be leaving in about an hour."

"But you'll arrive after dark. Should you wait and drive up tomorrow?" She always worried about him making the drive at night.

"I'll be fine Mom! I'll take the 79 up and 90 over. It won't take me long. and I'm familiar with the roads."

"What about Susan? Is she ok with that?"

He was dreading this conversation. "I'll see you soon Mom." He just couldn't do it on the phone.

He finished up the paperwork and went in search of Emily. He found her in the conference room finishing up a team pow wow.

"Hi. You're leaving?" she asked.

"Yea. Driving home to Rochester for the long weekend."

"You be careful driving at night!" she exclaimed, sincerely worried for him.

He laughed. "You sound like my mom."

"Yes, I'm that old," she laughed as well.

Have a wonderful holiday they both said in unison and laughed again. They hugged each other.

Tightly, Emily thought. He's not getting much physical contact these days. Then again, neither am I.

"Don't forget you are both taking over Casey's load while she's out on maternity leave starting Monday," the regional director, Tim, said to them before Kurt had a chance to get out of the room.

"I'll get with you Monday morning and we'll work it out," he said and walked out.

As he drove, he thought about it. The more he worked with Emily, the more he liked her. They'd known each other a long time and had always been professional friends.

He knew about the Ethics contract they signed, and they weren't allowed to date coworkers and yada yada, and it made sense. If things didn't work out, and it wasn't an amicable split, think of the stressful situation you would create in the work environment.

He didn't see that happening with Emily. She was mature and sensible. Any situation she was in, she managed with grace. That was part of what Kurt was most attracted to.

But they've never even been on a date. They have lunch together often. She dog sits for him. They've had coffee in her kitchen and tea on her patio, but that has been the extent of it.

But he liked her a lot. She was a soft spot in his life. They could easily talk and be comfortable together. He felt he could say anything to her.

A rest stop allowed Kurt and Martha to do their business, get drinks, and stretch their legs. A few hours later, Kurt arrived at the house of his childhood.

He loved coming home. Kurt's parents were loving and kind, and his childhood was happy. His memories here are good, with four siblings, him being smack in the middle, and they were a rowdy bunch, and he was encouraged to be so. His other siblings had families and were incredibly happy.

Mom and Dad met him at the door with big hugs and kisses. Once he settled Martha with her bed and blanket in the living room, he made his way to the kitchen, where a hot cup of tea awaited him. He heard Dad saying, "Now don't push him," as he entered the room.

"Sit down and have some tea. So, tell us now, what happened with Susan?"

"Well, that's not being pushy," Dad jumped on her.

"I'm just stating the obvious. I'm sure he wants to talk about it. Don't you?"

She patted his hand as she sat down, making him feel safe.

"Yes, I do," he stated matter-of-factly. "Susan and I broke off our relationship shortly after coming back from Hawaii. We just learned we were not looking for the same things. I can't be in a dead-end relationship now. I want marriage and kids. I want to see my kids graduate from college. I'm running out of time."

"Well, at least you haven't given up. The right one will come along." Dad said encouragingly, "If you keep an open mind."

"Your dad and I married incredibly young and had a family right away. It's not like that today. Kids are waiting 'until the right one comes along.' We fell in love, and whatever came along, we worked it out. It helped that we wanted the same things in life. That is important."

"I don't want to be the downer this weekend. When is everyone else coming in?" Kurt wanted the conversation to be over.

"Friday," Mom said. "The girls have all kinds of egg coloring and egg hunts planned."

She still called the women in the family girls, though they are in their thirties and forties.

"I can't wait!" Kurt was feeling better about everything. "I can't wait to see my nieces and nephews. They are the reason I am so good at my job."

"Well, you've got enough of them to practice on," Dad said, and they all laughed.

Kurt said good night and went up to his room. Martha followed him. The entire family went to church Sunday morning, and though getting all the kids ready in time was a challenge, the Holden clan made it happen.

The Methodist church they had gone to since birth was not big, and the Holden family took up the first three rows.

After services, they all went back to the house for a huge Easter dinner of ham, scalloped potatoes, corn, biscuits, and a buffet of pies and baskets full of candy.

The day was cool and sunny. Kurt helped hide the eggs for the hunt, then helped the little ones find them. His heart was full, and he didn't want the day to end.

"You don't want to leave too late and drive home in the dark," Mom said to everyone as they were packing up the cars, hugging all around; no one wanted to leave.

"We'll see you all this summer for the reunion," Dad said, waving goodbye.

Chapter 14 – Rishat's Vacation

Easter being the most festive event in India for Christians, Kumar decided they would travel to Mumbai for celebrations. He knew Rishat was struggling with her faith and thought this would help. Jaya came home and traveled with them by train.

"It will be about a three-hour trip, and we could spend the weekend there for Good Friday to Easter Sunday," he told Jaya at dinner on Wednesday.

"This sounds like an exciting adventure," Rishat said.

When they made plans for her to come home on spring break instead of going to a get-together of friends, Jaya told them, "But I wanted to visit some of my friends while I'm home."

"There'll be plenty of time for that. You'll be home for a week. Let's do this. Your father is so excited for it."

Rishat was excited about this, too, and had everything packed and ready for the trip on Thursday evening. They left early Friday morning.

Since this was a fasting day, they did not have to worry about packing food, only bottled water and light snacks.

Jaya and Kumar brought books to read, and Rishat just looked out the window and watched the scenery go by.

It was a spiritual awakening to see all the flowers and trees coming to life. She felt a fullness being with her family, and she liked that.

Mumbai was very crowded, and it was a good thing Kumar made reservations far ahead of time for a room.

They stayed at the JW Marriot Mumbai Sahar, which offered shuttles to the events in the area.

"We can also take buses to get around the city," Kumar said.

"Look how beautiful!" Rishat could not believe the elaborate extent they went to for this holiday.

The churches were adorned with decorations, and they were able to attend services that afternoon, followed by a special traditional drink prepared for everyone.

"India's diversity brings people of various religions together during Easter, with family and friends enjoying the festivities," Kumar told them. "It's a time to share a special bond of faith."

Kumar hoped this would provide some encouragement. Rishat felt full of hope in this place and time.

Saturday, they spent time in the shops and on the streets, getting the full experience of the celebration, buying decorative eggs as gifts of remembrance.

On Easter Sunday, they ate a special Easter brunch in the café at the hotel before boarding the train to return home. The weekend had gone by quickly. They were tired and slept mostly the entire ride home.

They no sooner got in the door, and Jaya was off to visit old friends. She had bought some decorative eggs as gifts to pass out to the families. One she had bought for herself, she put on her dresser before leaving.

"See you later," she called to Rishat and Kumar as she flew out the door.

They looked at each other and laughed at their daughter, but they loved her outgoing spirit and were proud of her accomplishments.

Kumar went to his computer to do some work as Rishat unpacked. She couldn't wait to tell Emily about her vacation.

Someone will have to get Cujo from the shelter.

Chapter 15 – Jaya

Jaya couldn't get out of the apartment fast enough. The weekend vacation with her parents had made her feel anxious and smothered. She knew her parents were not getting along well these days, and the tension in the house was sometimes unbearable.

But the weekend being together on the long train ride and the small hotel room had been too much. They barely talked to each other, and both talked mostly to her. She tried her best to give them equal time and keep them both happy.

She ran out the door almost as soon as they got home. She was grateful to have her own vehicle, purchased for her as a gift for convocation, so she could come and go whenever she wanted to.

At Trisha's house, she confided in her friend, "I felt like I was a buffer between them. If I had not been there, what would have become of them? I love my parents so much, but I don't want to be in the middle. What will happen if they divorce? How will we all get through it?"

Trisha felt bad for Jaya. Her own parents were happy, and she did not understand what Jaya was going through, but she still tried to offer comfort to her.

"I know this must be hard for you," she said to Jaya. "Maybe they will work it out. You don't know what will happen."

"I think they have been staying together for me. Now that I am at university, they have no reason to. It's feels like a matter of time." Jaya's eyes were teary.

Jaya stayed at Trisha's until late. When she went home, her parents were asleep in bed. First thing in the morning, after breakfast, she said goodbye to them with big hugs for both.

She took her time driving back to the university to relax and enjoy the spring day. She loved that she could be independent and make her own schedule, with no one looking over her, telling her to study, go to class, or don't you have a test coming up. Her mother had a good heart but felt the need to push Jaya to always be better. Jaya knew she had to keep her grades up, but she could relax and work at her own pace now.

She arrived in the late afternoon and didn't have a class until the next day. Her roommate was not back from the holiday break. In fact, most of the students had not come back yet. None of her friends were around. She felt lonely in her room.

She was caught up on her schoolwork but had an exam coming up in a week, so she decided to walk to the university library to study for a while. The place was empty, feeling eerie and even more lonely.

An hour later, she grabbed a mocha at the coffee shop on the way back to her room. Sharma was there and chattering away about her trip home to visit her family and see all her friends from school.

Jaya was glad to just listen to the happy stories, forgetting her sadness about her home situation.

Chapter 16 – Emily's Easter

Emily arrived at the adoration service on Holy Thursday promptly at 7:00 pm. She got her candle and found a seat.

She decided not to walk in the EM procession since she had not participated in the Eucharistic ministry in a long while. And she hadn't made it to confession.

The washing of the feet always made her cry, no matter who was participating. And after Holy Thursday service the tradition is to leave in silence. The experience always left Emily feeling emotional and filled with the spirit.

The calm that came over her was endearing and this year overwhelming.

Since she was struggling with her faith, the idea of a God dying on the cross for her was a lot to absorb.

She had no husband or family. No parents. She didn't even know where her brother was.

She couldn't find him when their mother died, so he wasn't able to come to her funeral. She couldn't forgive herself for not trying harder with him. After all, he lived in that house too, with all that heartache and lack of emotional love.

She was fasting, so there was no dinner on Thursday until services on Friday afternoon. She had a light dinner on Friday, and when Sunday came, she went to church on Easter morning.

The Church was very crowded (holiday Catholics) and many of her acquaintances were happy to see her.

"When are you coming back?" was the general question.

Coming back to where? As though the church is a home of some kind.

At one point in her life, she did think of church as her home. Had her faith been strong, or did she just need to have that safety net, thinking that would save her from all the sins?

Emily really hadn't led that bad a life, sin-wise.

I wouldn't consider myself a Jezabel or anything.

So, she'd had a few failed relationships. She put her mother in a home. She abandoned her little brother.

Stop thinking about this and beating yourself up. You are just bringing yourself down.

The Butterflies were having a brunch on Easter Sunday at the Cracker Barrell in New Stanton. She decided at the last minute to join them.

At least she would not have to cook; she didn't have anything to cook anyway, and some good company would do her good.

The food and conversation were very enjoyable. After eating, she went for a drive in the mountains to a place called Flat Rock in Linn Run State Park.

She walked along the stream, flowing briskly from the rain the day before, embracing the flow of the water, sounding fresh and crisp.

She needed this back-to-nature experience to renew her spirit. It always worked.

She then drove home and spent the rest of the afternoon watching movies.

That night, before bed, she received an email from Rishat talking about her faith crisis, telling Emily about how she celebrated the Holy Days and her own Easter Sunday experience.

"We are so on the same wavelength it's actually scary," she responded in messenger. "I am just getting into bed. I'll write to you soon."

Emily tossed and turned, wishing she could pick up the phone and call Rishat. Her heart ached for that closeness, and she wanted more now from this relationship.

But she knew these feelings were wrong and selfish.

She just celebrated the most religious holiday, and it made her aware of what God expected of her.

Delay gratification. Deny yourself and the sins of the flesh. You can say no.

This is a message Emily instructed her kids in therapy all the time. You don't have to have everything you want when you want it. This applied to everything from sex to alcohol and drugs, any worldly desire.

Wait! Say no!

This thought of living in the moment denies us the opportunity to reflect and understand what our heart tells us. Spend some time thinking about what you really want. And what the consequences are overall.

Emily got up and ate a bowl of honeycomb. She felt tired enough to go to sleep now, and she must have been out as soon as she hit the pillow because, what seemed like a minute later, the alarm went off. It was 8:00 am. She needed to get to work.

When she arrived at the center, the first thing she did was go to Kurt's office.

"How was your weekend?" he asked when she knocked and opened the door, not waiting for a response from him to stick her head in.

"Great," she said.

"You don't sound enthusiastic about it."

"I did not sleep well," she said. "Have you got the files we need to split?"

"Yes. Actually, I took my favorites and left you the rest," he chuckled, picking up a stack of folders and handed them to her.

"Gee. Thanks." She rolled her eyes and took the folders. "Are you free for dinner?" she surprised him and herself with the question.

"Ah. Yes. What did you have in mind," he was floored. That was going to be his move.

"I really need someone to talk to, sort of bounce something off of, and I don't want to talk here. The walls have ears."

He knew what she meant. "My last client is at 4:00. I can wrap up the paperwork and be able to leave around 5:00. Will that work for you?"

"I'll check my calendar when I get to my office, but I'm sure I can make it work. Thanks for getting a jump on this," she held up the file folders he had given her. "See ya later."

At 5:00, Kurt knocked on Emily's door, "Ready?"

"As a matter of fact, I am," she said. "Any idea where to go."

"How about the Pour House in town? I'll drive."

They got in his car, and as he drove, he talked on and on about his weekend, his family, and his fun with the kids. They got a parking space right in front. There was no one there so they had their pick of tables.

Once they ordered drinks, Emily began, "I need to find my brother."

"I didn't know you had a brother," to his surprise, Emily got tears in her eyes. *I've never seen that before.*

How sad is it that no one even knows I have a brother. She stopped herself from crying.

The waiter brought their drinks two glasses of red wine, and asked if they were ready to order. They both ordered steaks, medium rare, with a baked potato and no sour cream.

"Are you copying me?" Kurt asked, trying to lighten the mood. She laughed. He felt better.

"I don't even know where to start," she hesitates for a minute, then dives right in. "I have a brother. I haven't seen him since my father died. When my mom got sick, he didn't want anything to do with her care. I moved her into a nursing facility, sold the family home, and never spoke to him again."

She paused to take a sip of her wine, trying to read Kurt's face to see if he was judging her. But she knew he would not do that. It was just her guilt getting to her.

She continued, "The last I heard, he was living with a woman, working at a garage, and going to mechanic's school. Then I think he got fired, his girlfriend went to jail or something."

She took another sip of wine, "I know you collaborate with juveniles sometimes, and I don't know if you can even help me, but you are the one person I can ask."

"Well, he is not a juvenile. How old would he be now?"

"He is three years younger than me, which would make him 29," she had to do the math.

"Okay. What's his name?"

"Samual Peterson. Sammy," tears were pouring down her face now. "I haven't even said his name in all these years. I didn't even try to reach him when my mom died. I had no idea where to look for him, so I didn't even try. Then, when I saw about his girlfriend and the drug bust, I thought he was in on that."

Kurt rubbed her arm and let her calm down before he asked any more questions.

When their steaks came, Emily excused herself to wash up in the bathroom. Once alone, she washed her face and got herself calmed down.

When she returned, they ate quietly for a while, Emily pushing her food around her plate, barely tasting it when she did take a bite.

Kurt resumed the conversation.

"How's your steak? Done the way you like it?" he asked casually.

"Yes. It's delicious! How about yours?" she replied.

"Absolutely delicious!" they laughed, and the air was breathable again.

"Emily, I'm sure you did the best you could with the situation. Taking care of a sick mother is a lot. And feeling like you're alone in that is hard. I will look into some things and see if I can get some information about him. Do you have his girlfriend's name? How about any high school friends he may still be in touch with?"

"See! I would never have thought about that. I'll try to dig out some information and get it to you. Thank you so much for your help and for not judging me."

"It sounds like you are judging yourself enough for the both of us. Stop that!"

"K," more crying.

Chapter 17 – Sammy

On Easter Sunday, Sammy had found a Catholic church to attend mass. He was embarrassed about his appearance, so he had gone into the local shelter to find a suit to borrow.

Washed up and dressed up, he actually looked rather good, but he still sat in the back pew to avoid people. He didn't smell great, and the old suit was dingy and didn't fit well.

He remembered, as a child, being in church with his mom, dad, and Emily and it made him hurt inside. He wondered how people who went to church every Sunday could be so mean, cold, and unaffectionate.

He thought with this suit he might be able to find a job and get back on his feet. But any establishment he applied to would need a current driver's license and he did not have the money to renew it. Nor did he have an address to put on it, which was also required.

It was a catch-22. How did the government expect anyone to get out of this rut when they make it as hard as they can with all these laws?

"It's necessary to protect the people from fraud and identity theft and all the other crimes people commit to scam everyone," one of the guys around the fire barrel had said when they were discussing it one night.

"The government scams us more than we scam each other."

He had laughed, but Sam knew he was blowing off the booze and didn't really have a clue what he was talking about. He offered Sam his bottle, and Sam turned him down flat.

Sammy didn't drink or take drugs. "It's hard enough just getting food without risking going to jail for that stuff." He told him.

"At least in jail, we'd have a warm bed, food, and all the comforts of home."

Now Sammy knew he was crazy.

"You also have to watch your back every minute of every day. I just don't think like that," he said, moving on to find another place to hang out. He couldn't let his mind start to think that way.

"Good luck to ya!" the guy called after him.

That's when Sammy decided to go to church.

Sitting in the back pew, Sammy knelt and put his head in his praying hands.

God, please help me. Help me get out of this

situation. I'm lost, and I don't know the way. Show me the way, Lord.

Tears began pouring out, and he sobbed.

The man in front of him turned and asked, "You okay, son?"

The sobbing got worse, and he got up to leave. The man followed Sammy out and tried to stop him, but Sammy was too ashamed.

"Please just take my card," he caught up and handed it to him. "I'm a counselor here at the church, and I want to help you. Please call me."

Sammy took the card and ran off in the direction of the river, heading for a bridge.

Chapter 18 – Rishat

When Rishat opened the latest email from Emily, she was pleasantly surprised.

My sweet lady,

You don't know the effect you are having on my life now. I think about you all the time and wonder what you are doing in that moment.

I lay in bed at night, wishing you were here to comfort and embrace me. The loneliness has made me desire you in a way I never knew I could.

My Easter weekend was difficult because it reminded me of my faith and commitment to God. I am called to follow his word, but I am resisting because it means giving up something I want.

I know we are called not to follow the ways of the world, to sacrifice ourselves for the good of others. To be good stewards and lead others to Him. I cannot be a leader in my church if I do not follow those beliefs.

I want so much to bring you here and fulfill these desires I have for you. The emotional love is overwhelming, but the physical act of that love means to give up everything I believe is good and right in God's eyes.

I am so torn. If I did not care about our different beliefs and faith this would not be such a struggle. I cannot ask you to walk away from what you have there, to let go of your husband and daughter, to walk away from what you have spent your life building and to live in sin.

I'm sure this struggle is real for all those who make the decision to be together in this way. If two people genuinely love each other, with the love of Christ, not arrogance or defiance, but true heartfelt love, how can it be sinful?

It is so hard to know what is right. We can only live the way we do and know there is a plan for our lives in God's eyes.

Where does that leave us, Rishat?

Attending church on Easter Sunday brought to my conscience many issues needing healing. I am trying to find my brother. I have not spoken to him since my father died.

God is calling me to heal this relationship. My coworker, Kurt, is helping me. This will change my life in a big way, I think, but it's something I must do.

I want you to think about all I have said here very sincerely. Our decisions about moving forward will affect many people around us.

My eyes are on India. And you. With all my heart!

Em

Rishat's heart was filled with emotion. When she finished reading this, tears were pouring down her cheeks. She knew now she shared Emily's feelings, and she also shared her struggle with them.

Emily knew exactly what Rishat's thoughts were before Rishat even had to tell her. This was the connection they had that was strong.

They needed to slow down and really examine the consequences of the choice they would be making now.

Jaya had just started her journey away from home into adult life.

Whatever Rishat chose would have the biggest impact on her for she would want Jaya to come to America with her. There would be so many more opportunities available to her. How could she pass up that chance?

Kumar would be fine. He had already disconnected from Rishat in his heart. He would just have to disconnect his mind from her. She didn't think that would take long. There were many women looking for good men like him. He could move on easily.

But then Rishat thought, he is a good man. *Do I really want to leave him? Would I be going to something better?*

The stigma of divorce is bad enough then to go into a gay relationship. However, America is more accepting of this process than India.

But all the years she invested in her marriage. It wasn't perfect but it was comfortable, and she fit into a society that would respect her in this station of life, especially with her work with the kids.

I am a righteous woman with a husband and child. There is no scandal in my past. How could I bring this on, Kumar?

But Kumar hadn't touched her in over a year. And she wanted a loving marriage. She wanted intimacy. Not a charade. It was a lot to think about. She replied to Emily via messenger:

My love, I share your emotions and struggles. I will need to take time to process all of this. It may take a while. Please don't think I'm ignoring you. I will respond when I can honestly address this relationship with you from my heart.

Emily sent a heart emoji back immediately. Rishat understood what that meant, and she appreciated the understanding gesture of patience. She was giving her space.

Chapter 19 – A Church in Pittsburgh

Drew Mangeli walked into the office of the pastor of the church on Monday afternoon two weeks following Easter Mass. He felt it was long enough to wait.

"Has a boy called looking for me?" he asked Father Martin, who was on his computer working on the bulletin for the following week.

"I used to count on my secretary to do this, but with the cutbacks, she barely has time to do much when she is here," he turned away and gave Drew his attention. "What boy would that be?" he asked.

"On Easter Sunday, I was extremely late due to a personal reason, and the church was packed so I had to sit in the back."

"I wondered why I didn't see you."

"Yes. Well, this boy was sitting behind me, sobbing into his hands. I turned and asked if he was okay. It was that intense. He got up quickly and ran out. I chased after him and gave him a business card, telling him to please call me."

"Why would he call me then?" Father was confused.

"Well, he hasn't called me, and I guess I was hoping that if he'd maybe lost my card, he might have called the church, you, or someone here."

"Nope. I haven't heard from him or gotten any messages that a boy was trying to reach you. Was he young?"

"Not really, maybe late twenties, but he was definitely homeless. I recognized the suit he had on as one of the shelter loans out to men going on job interviews."

"Maybe that's where you should start looking, at the shelters, if you're that determined to pursue it."

"I am that determined. And that is a good idea. Thank you, Father. Get back to your bulletin."

Father Martin grumbled. Drew smiled and walked out.

He wasn't sure why he was being called to this, but he knew there was a reason. The delay getting to church was a fluke, spilling his coffee down the front of his suit, forcing him to change, having to sit in the back row due to no seats available that late, the boy sitting right behind him.

The Holy Spirit is working here. He knew it sure as he knew anything. Light of Life Rescue on Voeghtly St was the only shelter that offered suits, so he decided to start there.

The young girl behind the entrance desk wore a name tag that said, Heather.

"Hi, Heather," Drew said as he approached the counter she sat behind. "I'm looking for a kid who may have borrowed a suit from your shelter for Easter Sunday. Is that something you can help me with?"

"You should talk to David. He would be the one to take care of that," she picked up her phone receiver and buzzed. "Dave, there's a man out here wanting to talk with you."

She hung up and said, "He'll be right out."

David Graham, who was the manager of the men's program, came out a few minutes later, walking right up to Drew and shaking his hand. "I'm Dave. How can I help you?"

"Hi, Dave," Drew extended his hand. "I'm Drew Mangeli. I am a youth counselor for a church in Pittsburgh. I am looking for a young man who borrowed a suit for Easter Sunday. Do you all keep records of who you lend suits to?"

"Nope. Everything's confidential here. No last names, no records. If they bring back the suit, okay. If not, we get more suits. We get a lot donated in various sizes, so we don't need to get them back."

"But if you did loan a suit to someone, you'd know

who, like his first name or something?"

"Not really. And if I did, I couldn't tell you anyway. Some guys only come for meals, but we don't interact much with them or see them back here in the offices. Unless they ask for counseling with me, I don't see them again."

"Okay. Thanks!" He turned to leave, then had a second thought. He walked back and handed Dave his card. "If you hear of anything about a kid in church on Easter Sunday. I don't know. I'm grasping here." He shrugged and left.

Drew decided to give up. He knew he'd get the same speech no matter where he went.

That night at home, he ate dinner in the living room in front of the television, watching the news.

The number of homeless in Pittsburgh was increasing every day. And now, with all the killings, at times, it filled him with despair.

His only escape was to do the work that kept him in the loop, trying to get these kids on the right track before they fell off the grid. Once they were gone, it was ten times harder to get them back.

He put his dish in the sink and took Josh, his German Shepherd, for a walk. He didn't wear the right jacket, and he was cold.

Chapter 20 – Kurt

"With the workload from Casey being out and keeping up with my own, I haven't had much time to follow up with this," he explained to Emily when she came into his office the following week.

Kurt hadn't even seen her since their dinner, and she seemed to be avoiding him. He wondered if she felt uncomfortable now by confiding this in him.

"It's okay. I'm bogged down too, and that's what I wanted to tell you. Please don't feel pressure to do anything with my problem right now. We have too much going on. I haven't even had time to look up any of his old friends and that was a great suggestion. But I will do what I can when I can and don't want you to feel obligated."

"Well, I can tell you that I looked at the jails and asked around about the girlfriend and it doesn't seem that he participated in that bust. He's not in jail," he saw she was tearing up, and though that was good news, it still brought an emotional response, naturally so.

"Thank you. I have some clients waiting but thank you so much. That means a lot," she bolted out the door and was gone.

Kurt didn't know how to handle this emotional Emily and he had been avoiding her as well. He even found himself eating lunch in his office, so he didn't run into her in the employee lounge.

She had always been so sensible and in control. This side of her made him uncomfortable. But he did want to help her find her brother. In all the time he had known her, to see her acting this way now meant it had to be important to her. She wouldn't be reacting this way if it weren't.

After jail, his next thought was the homeless shelters.

Obviously, he's off the grid. He has no cell phone, no address, no job. Common sense says homeless if he's still in this area. Or he just doesn't want to be found.

He had about twenty minutes till his next client came in. He googled homeless shelters in Pittsburgh. The first one to come up, a big one, was the Light of Life Rescue Mission. He picked up the phone to call.

"Light of Life," a voice said on the other end.

"Hi. My name is Kurt Holden. I'm a psychologist at County Mental Health Hospital in Greensburg. This is going to sound like a weird request, but I'm looking for a kid named Sammy Peterson. I wonder if he has been to this shelter. Is there someone I can talk to about this?"

"One moment, please."

Click. Click. Ringing.

"Light of Life, Dave speaking."

"Hi. My name is Kurt Holden. I'm a psychologist at the County Mental Health Hospital in Greensburg. I'm looking for a kid named Sammy Peterson. I wonder if he has been to this shelter."

"Well, being a psychologist, you would know that the information you are asking for is confidential."

"Yes, I do know that." He had that coming. "But family is trying to find him for urgent reasons, and we have checked the jails. My next thought was to check the shelters. I know it's a long shot, but here's the deal; you don't have to tell me if he is coming there or if you know him, but could you at least pass on the information if you do see him? However discrete you can be, let him know his sister is looking for him."

"I will tell you there was a man here a few days ago looking for someone named Sammy. Claimed he saw him at a church in Pittsburgh on Easter Sunday. He left me his name and number. I guess it'd be okay if I give you that information."

Kurt wrote down the number Dave gave him for Drew Mangeli and gave Dave his own information as well.

"Look! We're trying to get a family together here. If the kid's homeless, he could need her now. Let's help him out."

He hung up and realized his next client had been waiting in the playroom for ten minutes.

Apologizing profusely, he greeted them and walked them back to his office.

He had to focus on his work now and put this stuff aside for Emily. He couldn't let it affect his work. He'd call her later at home and tell her about this new breakthrough.

She's gonna cry.

Chapter 21 – Emily

Emily knew what she had done. Rishat was going to have a difficult time processing all Emily had disclosed to her about her feelings.

I can't even imagine what she must be thinking.

Though they had been friends on Facebook for years, it had only been a few months since they had been exchanging conversations and getting to know each other intimately.

She thought of Richard and Paul, two men in her hiking group who had been coming for a year.

She watched them as their relationship progressed. They spent time slowly getting to know each other, walking and talking, ignoring everyone around them. You could see them falling in love, softly, gently, respectfully, without regret.

Emily never talked to them on a personal level, so she knew nothing of their character. Did they have a faith they struggled with? What was their family situation like?

She only knew they were not arrogant or conceded in any way and they didn't flaunt the relationship boldly in everyone's face. It touched her heart deeply.

This is love. There has to be a purpose. A plan. We don't have all the answers. We don't know what God's will in anyone's life will be.

Emily's phone rang out the song Bridge Over Troubled Water, her ringtone for Kurt. Pulling herself out of the funk she was in, she answered.

"Hey, did I wake you?" he asked. "You sound kind of groggy."

"No, I was just sitting here reading my last email from Rishat. We are having some emotional bonding issues, and I haven't heard from her in a while, so I am worried she's not processing well. I don't know if that makes sense."

"You are juggling a lot of balls here, aren't you?" Now he knew why she was crying so much.

"Maybe I'm having a mid-life crisis," she speculated.

They both laughed.

"Hey, we got a laugh!" He was happy to hear it. "But you're far from midlife."

"Not that far."

"Well, I got some more news that may make you even happier. I talked with the Light of Life Rescue today, the homeless shelter in Pittsburgh, and I told them we were looking for Sammy. He said someone else had been in there looking for a Sammy. A youth counselor at a church in Pittsburgh. The counselor said Sammy sat behind him at church on Easter Sunday. I'm not sure of the whole story or if this is even our Sammy, but it's weird. Might turn into something. Anyway, I left my name and number in case he heard anything else."

The phone was quiet. He waited.

"Kurt, I can't thank you enough for helping me," she finally said. "I would never have gotten as far as you have. I didn't even know where to start. You are the best guy I know. Really! You are!"

"Really? The best?" he asked, and she laughed again.

He continued, "Thanks! That means a lot to me. I haven't been getting a lot of attention or affection lately and I'm sort of running on empty half the time. The only nurturing I'm getting is from my mom, who calls at least twice a week."

"But you got a mom who calls you. And I'll bet she says, 'I love you' a lot, too, doesn't she?" Emily was teasing him, but he knew there was an underlying envy and sadness there.

"Yes, she does," he said, feeling bad for her now and wanting to end this conversation before she started to cry again. "So hey, I'll let you know if I hear anything more, but I'm kind of at a dead end here. We've planted some seeds. Let's see where it goes."

She hung up and thought about messaging Rishat but decided not to. She promised to give her space and time to make this decision. It was a huge, life-changing move to make.

Emily wasn't positive she was ready to make this move either. She did know one thing. If they went through this struggle, and decided, whatever Rishat's choice is, it was a solid commitment. And Emily would live with that, through thick and thin.

"There's a lot of waiting going on here," she said to Spot.

Spot meowed that she, too, was waiting … for dinner.

Chapter 22 – Sammy

It had been weeks, and Sammy hadn't returned the suit. It was looking pretty shabby by now.

The bridge was a bust. Too many cars going by and beeping. No one stopped to offer help. One car slowed down, and a young woman hung out the window saying, "Why would you kill yourself on Easter Sunday, man?"

After that, he hung out with the rest of the homeless community, lying around all day, building a fire at night, and scavenging for food at the restaurants when they could.

He hadn't eaten in days. He decided to go to the shelter, turn in the suit to get his clothes back (they keep them in a bag with your name on it), and maybe ask to talk to someone. One of the counselors there.

He knew that service was available but never took advantage of it. He figured, what was the point? There really wasn't anything they could do. Loan you a suit, listen to your pain, and encourage you to keep a good faith and cheerful outlook.

What was the point?

Sammy arrived at the Light of Life and walked into the lobby, where a receptionist was sitting behind a counter.

"Can I help you?" she asked when she saw him come in and looked like he didn't know what to do.

"I want to return this suit. I borrowed it several weeks ago and haven't had a chance to get over here to return it."

She picked up the phone, "Dave, there's a man here wanting to return the suit he borrowed a couple weeks ago." She said.

"Can you do the return for me? I'm knee-deep in this paperwork and feel like I can't breathe."

"It's not in my job description," she said. "I'm not going into the men's shower room."

"He'll be right out," she said to Sammy, hung up the phone, and went back to her computer to finish her solitaire game.

Sammy walked around the lobby, looking at the pictures, figurines, and memorabilia about not giving up, and keep believing in yourself. There was a crucifix on one wall and a picture of Jesus on another.

Sammy was getting impatient when Dave finally came out.

"Hi, son. You're returning the suit?" Dave saw the suit was in pretty bad shape and wondered why he even came back. Maybe the clothes he'd left here were better.

"Yeah. Thanks," Sammy got up and followed David back to the area that looked like a dressing area.

There were showers, towels, and bars of soap available for anyone who borrowed the suits to make themselves acceptable for job interviews.

"What's your name son?" Dave asked.

"Sam," he said, wishing he'd stop calling him son.

"How was the interview?" Dave asked as he searched the drawers for a bag with the name Sam on it.

"I didn't have an interview," he said.

Dave found a bag with the name Sammy on it. Something pulled at the back of his mind, but he couldn't remember.

"Sammy? Here it is. We always have the clothes washed to give back to you. So, do you want to take a shower?" he asked.

Sammy thought a shower would be a good idea. He was handed his bag of clean clothes, with a towel and a small bar of soap.

"When you're finished, put the suit and towel in the wash container, and throw the soap away unless you want to keep it. If you need anything else, I'll be in my office."

"Thanks!" Sammy was profoundly grateful. He spent a long time letting the hot water wash over him, soaping up, rinsing off, and soaping up again. He felt like he couldn't get the dirt off.

Finally, he dried off, threw the old clothes and towel in the wash can, which was actually a garbage can with a lid, and walked down the long hall to the lobby.

As he walked by Dave's office, he waved a thanks and goodbye to him. Dave waved for him to come in, so he opened the door and put his head in.

"Hey. You're welcome to go down to the kitchen and grab a bag lunch to take with you. The girls down there can help you. Just tell them you talked to me."

"Thanks!"

In the lobby, the girl behind the desk was MIA. He assumed a bathroom run. Shame! He felt like a fresh person when he walked out and thought he might have a chance to talk with her. Then again, she probably gets that a lot.

As he went out the door and down the sidewalk, he didn't know why, but something felt different.

Suddenly, he heard Dave running up behind him, "Sam! Sammy! Is your name Sammy? That's what it said on the bag."

He turned and saw a piece of paper in his hand, "Yea. That's what my sister always called me."

When Dave heard him say sister, he knew he had the right kid, "Did you go to a church in Pittsburgh on Easter Sunday?"

"Yes! That's what the suit was for," Sammy said.

"People have been looking for you. Something about a family situation. This counselor from the church came and said if you showed up to, give you this message.

Another guy called, too, a psychologist from somewhere, but I can't find his info. I told them I didn't know you. Well, here's the number. Do what you want with it."

Sammy took the piece of paper and shoved it in his pocket.

"Thanks," he said, walking away.

He didn't know what to think. What was going on? Why would anyone be trying to reach him due to a 'family situation.' Suddenly he worried about Emily. Was she okay?

Sammy walked back to the spot where he had been hanging with the homeless community. He didn't have any money to travel back to Greensburg. He didn't even have a way to call anyone. He sat all day wondering what to do.

When his stomach growled, he realized he forgot to grab his bagged lunch.

Chapter 23 – A Church in Pittsburgh

Drew was in the rectory talking with Father Martin about the upcoming summer programs for the youth group when Amy knocked on the door.

Amy was part-time and didn't really get much done, so it was rare to see her on a weekday afternoon. Usually, she was in the offices down at the school or in the cafeteria.

"Oh, Drew. Just the person I'm looking for. I was about to call you but thought I'd check with Father first to see where you might be," Amy said.

"What's up?" Drew exclaimed.

"Well, there's a young man out here who's been looking for you. Name's Sammy. He came down to the school thinking you'd be there. Says he was given your name and number by a counselor at the shelter."

"Where is he now?" Drew asked her, standing up quickly and walking out into the hallway.

"He's down at the school. I didn't want to bring him up here. He's pretty shabby looking."

"Amy!" Father Martin exclaimed. "We don't reject anyone because of how they look."

"Well, you know! The money's up here and everything. You just never know," she said defensively.

Drew had walked away from the conversation and went to the school. He walked into the main gathering area, where chairs and tables were set up for group meetings.

A young man sat at a table on the far end of the room. Drew recognized him from church. When he approached him, the boy stood and said, "I'm Sammy. Is my sister okay?"

"I don't know anything about that, but I do know she is looking for you. How long have you two been estranged from each other?"

"I don't know. A long time," he plopped back down in the seat and put his hands on his face on the table, sobbing again.

Drew sat down opposite him and waited. He could feel the pain this boy was in. His heart went out to him.

"Son," he said, finally breaking the silence. "A psychologist at the Community Mental Health Hospital is looking for you. Something about your family. I have his information. Would you like to call him?"

"Yes. I want to know if my sister's okay," Sammy

said, genuinely concerned now.

"Okay. How about we go to my place? We'll get you something to eat, and we'll call from the privacy of my home. Would that be okay?"

"Yes. Thank you!" Sammy followed Drew to his car, and they drove to his house on the east side of town.

When they entered, Drew immediately fed Josh. Sammy sat at the kitchen table watching Drew and Josh petting and interacting and thought how nice it would be to have a dog. They never had pets growing up.

Emily had that dachshund dad wanted to breed, but that was short-lived. The dog couldn't get pregnant or something and they ended up giving her away.

"So, let's see what I've got," Drew opened his frig and then his freezer. "I'm afraid I'm a typical bachelor. I have no food," he laughed. "How bout we order a pizza?"

"Sounds good!" Sammy said enthusiastically. He couldn't remember the last time he had a freshly made pizza that didn't have garbage all over it or the taste of mouse droppings.

With the pizza ordered and arriving in about 45 minutes, Drew needed to take Josh for a walk.

"Do you want to come or stay here and watch some

television till I get back?"

"I'll hang here if you don't mind," he said. He was pretty tired and didn't want to go walking anymore. He'd walked far enough. "When are we calling this guy you talked about."

"As soon as I get back, we'll try to reach him," Drew wanted to call at the hour when he thought he'd have a better chance of getting him on the phone.

"Psychologists always schedule appointments on the hour. I don't want to have to leave a message and wait for a callback. Make yourself at home. I'll be back in 30."

Sammy plopped down on the couch and turned on the television. He put some talk show on, and it wasn't long before he had nodded off.

He woke when Drew and Josh came in. The pizza came shortly after. While eating, Drew talked about how long he had lived in this old house, the work he did with the church and about the dog.

Sammy ate five pieces of pizza quickly and got a stomachache.

It was 3:00.

"So, let's make that call."

Chapter 24 – Kumar

Kumar felt something was off with Rishat. He knew their marriage had lost its passion but always thought her a sensible and committed partner.

If she were having an affair, he would be shocked. She just did not have that in her at all. And there were no signs of other men being in the picture.

But a cloud-like happiness had come over her. Like she was living in a fantasy, she seemed almost giddy sometimes. She blushed when he asked her about it one time.

"You have been so cheerful lately," he said to her.

"I am just feeling happy to have Jaya off to university and my new position at school to work with the kids. They are a joy," she had said.

He knew she went to the school and back with her workshops and how much she loved doing that. It would not have been her dream, but it seemed to satisfy her desire to teach.

Now, he was not sure what to think. She spent a long time on her computer when she was home and sometimes on her phone at night. Could she have met someone there online?

He didn't know how she could be meeting anyone in person. She never went out anywhere but for groceries in the market, taking Cujo for walks, or tutoring her students. She was always there and back.

With the stress of his job and his family needing him, he did not have the energy sometimes to give Rishat his time and affection.

He must pay for Jaya's university and see to her living needs. He spent long hours at work sometimes. That was all taking a toll on his marriage. When Jaya was home, it was not so hard because she was like a cushion between them. But now it was just the two of them.

Had they grown so much apart that they had nothing to talk about anymore? Were they bored with each other now?

They slept in twin beds and had not come together like that in over a year. She was never one to want the physical relationship so much.

After she discovered she could not have more children, she seemed to lose interest. She invested all her affection to Jaya.

He was unsure how to approach this subject with her. How to go about reconnecting now? This is a challenge he felt he had no energy to face. But he was not willing to lose his precious Rishat.

He had built a good relationship with Jaya, and they were remarkably close.

To find out about the difficulties in their marriage or, God forbid, they should get a divorce would be an enormous blow to her.

It was time for him to have a talk with Rishat and determine what was going on with her. He hoped she would open up and be honest with him, for all of this was about saving their marriage.

He picked up the phone and rang the number for Rishat. He wasn't sure of her schedule but hoped she'd answer. She did.

"Are you still at the school?" he asked.

"Yes. I am walking Cujo," Rishat said. "Where are you?"

"I am still here as well. I was wondering if you'd be available for dinner tonight," he asked, sounding sweet and personable, like flirting.

"You mean to go out and eat? Like at a restaurant?" She asked, surprised.

"Yes. We could go to Nutin. You like that place, right?"

"Oh! I love that restaurant! Is this like a date?"

"Yes! It will be like a date," he said, feeling a little

shy now.

"Well, I have Cujo and my car here. I will have to meet you at home."

"Yes! That would be good, actually. I'll pick you up at home, and we can go to dinner at Nutin. You've always liked the food there. It will be a treat."

"I love the food there. What time should I expect you to pick me up?" she asked extremely excited now.

"How about 6:00?" He could hear the excitement in her voice, and he knew this was a good idea.

"I will be ready."

They both felt a little awkward with this new kind of playful interaction.

He hung up, sure this was going to be a good decision. He rearranged his schedule to make sure he would be on time to pick her up.

He even had a spare shaver in his desk for occasions of importance, and he considered this important.

Freshly washed up and shaved, he left work to pick up his date. He felt an excitement he had not felt in a long time, too.

Chapter 25 – Rishat

She could barely contain herself. She got Cujo in the car and drove home directly, stopping only for fresh, smelly body lotion. She anticipated she may need it.

At home, Rishat took a bath using her body wash and prepared herself for a romantic evening. She looked in the mirror at her shoulder-length black hair. It is still thick and wavey. Her figure is full and shapely. Her face is not yet showing wear.

She felt good about herself. She picked a nice feminine dress from her closet. She didn't have many, nor did she have many occasions to wear one, so they all seemed new to her. She knew they would be appealing to Kumar also.

Wearing her hair down for a change and applying her makeup, she was ready. She sat to wait on him and fantasized about how the evening might go. This had not happened in so long that she wasn't even sure what to expect.

What brought this on? She didn't want to over think it. *Just relax and enjoy yourself in the moment!*

Rishat was watching the clock, and it made her anxious. She got on her phone to check her messages. She had not heard from Emily and knew Emily was waiting for an answer about coming to America to live. Why would she be thinking about her now?

There was a love there she could not deny. But she had a history of love with her husband, and she felt she needed to save her marriage.

Give him a chance.

And then there was a knock on the door. Rishat rose to answer it. Kumar stood in the doorway with a basket of flowers.

"I thought you might like this better than a bouquet that will die in a few days," he handed her the basket and said. "You look beautiful!"

She was overwhelmed, "Yes. I am ready."

She set the basket on the table, and they went out for dinner.

At the restaurant, Kumar was attentive and affectionate, holding her hand and looking at her when they talked. They even found new things to talk about, like the art in the restaurant and new movies coming out.

There was the sense of emotional intimacy that Rishat needed, that had been missing in their marriage for a long time. And Kumar opened up.

"I know we have not been close for a long time in our marriage. I don't know what happened to make the romance and emotional love go away, but it seems we just settled into this comfortable relationship that was just about responsibilities and commitments. But there is no fun in us anymore. I realized it over Easter, on vacation. When Jaya is with us, it is either you and her or me and her, like you and I don't exist anymore. Rishat, I want to have fun with you. I want us to be together like when we were first married. We looked forward to being together. I know your life didn't turn out exactly the way you wanted, but was it so bad that you are very unhappy with me now?"

"I grew to love you, Kumar. And I have been incredibly happy building our home and raising our daughter. No life is not what I would have chosen, but it has been good. You are good. I like being your wife. I like that we are respected in our community. I don't want us to lose that either."

"I am so happy to hear you say that. I have been worried that you had found someone else. Let's rekindle our love for each other and put this behind us."

"I would love that too."

Rishat's struggle was put to rest that minute. She resolved to stay where she was and continue to try to build a good marriage. She hoped this would be a message to Jaya also about making a life with a husband and family.

It was good and right. That night, at home, Kumar came into Rishat's bed, and they made love.

As they cuddled after, Kumar said, "How about tomorrow we go shopping for a double bed?"

"We will be a modern couple, as Jaya would say."

They both laughed.

Chapter 26 – Kurt

Kurt wrapped up his 2:00 session a few minutes early and sat at this desk inputting the information from the session into his computer database he kept on all his clients.

This one he just finished is a difficult case, abandoned at three, in and out of foster care, a behavioral problem at school, and on meds that weren't being taken as prescribed, not for lack of the foster parents trying.

He always tried to think positively and never liked to give up on a kid, but he just wasn't sure how this one was going to turn out. Once that self-destruct pattern is established, it is hard to bring them back.

The early child development years are a main factor. What the child learns during these years is what they continue throughout their lives. It's what they've learned, it's all they know. The pattern is so hard to break.

As he was typing in his evaluation, his phone rang. When he answered he was surprised by the voice on the other end.

"Hello. Is this Kurt Holden?" the voice asked.

"Yes. How can I help you?"

"My name is Sammy Peterson. I understand you are looking for me."

Sammy's voice was cracking as he spoke. He knew something was going on with his sister and he wasn't sure it was going to be good.

"Hi Sam. How are you?" Kurt said.

He didn't exactly know how to start so he delayed a bit.

"Is my sister, okay?" was all Sammy wanted to know.

"Your sister's fine Sam. I am her coworker. She asked for my help to find you. She says you two have been estranged for a long time and she wants to reconnect with you. Is that something you are interested in doing, Sammy?"

There was silence for a moment, so Kurt continued, "If not, this call can end, and this all goes away. I don't have to tell her I found you. You can make a choice to see her when you're ready. It's all in your control."

"Nothing has ever been in my control," he said, and Kurt could tell he was on the verge of crying.

"Well, this is." Kurt simply said. He knew it was going to be hard for him to keep this from Emily if he chose not to see her, but right now Sammy's needs are more important.

"Can I think about it. You're sure Em's okay?"

"Yes. She is fine. You can reach me at this number when you are ready to decide. If I don't hear from you, I will respect your privacy and wish you well. But Sammy, know that Emily loves you and misses you. And wants a reconciliation very much."

"Bye." Is all he said, and he was gone.

Now Kurt had to let it go too. He made a promise and would keep it. It was out of his control. If Emily ever found out, she'd have to understand.

Being a counselor herself, she knows all about confidentiality. But somehow, it's harder when it applies to you.

Emily had never confided much in him about the dynamics of her family. He knew she left home at eighteen and put herself through school.

She always seemed like a very loving kind person, but sometimes a person who has been deprived of that emotional presence growing up would tend to overcompensate by being that way toward others.

We give what we don't get.

Since Kurt came from such a loving, happy family, his expectations were pretty high.

He began to realize he had a hard time with emotional women. *Why?* He didn't remember his mother being emotional. She was a rock.

 Therefore, should all women be rocks? Without emotion.

He remembered how annoyed he was when Susan was scared on the plane. Maybe he needed to change. Maybe he needed to look closer at this part of himself.

Something to think about.

Chapter 27 – Emily

Friday evening, Emily sat on the patio with her phone beside her. She knew she had an email from Rishat but was hesitating to open it.

Her feelings were so torn about what she wanted, but she knew what she didn't want, and that was to break up a marriage and family.

This has been such an emotional stress on her, as Kurt had said, she has a lot on her plate.

Whatever the response is from Rishat she is going to have to accept it and move forward now. Once the words had been spoken, there was no turning back.

Might as well get on with it.

She opened up her computer and began to read:

My dearest Emily,

My heart is so full of love for you. This decision is not an easy one because of that. I have been turning over all the consequences of the actions we will take now. No matter what direction we go in, the journey will not be easy.

I must tell you this, Kumar has come around to a complete turn in a direction I am excited about. Last week we had a date night and we connected in a way that we never had before.

We also had an intimate night and shared a bed for the first time in over a year. I am sorry if this news is hurtful to you. It is not my intent, just to be open and honest with you because you deserve it.

You are such a beautiful person in your mind and heart. I am genuinely sad to not be able to realize the relationship and act on the feelings of love we have.

As we both believe, all things are for the good of everyone and this I think is the best decision for my family.

I am an influence on my impressionable daughter and must be responsible for her wellbeing. She belongs here with her father.

The work I am doing with the kids at the school is so important to me also. I like that I am a respected teacher and role model for them.

It is hard today for kids to make choices about identity and relationships. I know you agree, being an example that is solid and consistent in values is important for a future generation.

We are so much alike in so many ways and that is why we bonded so quickly. You are my dearest friend and I know you played a big part in the transformation of my person and family. Indirectly, you changed me, which changed the way others see me.

I know we can still be pen-pals and offer each other support and encouragement in our journey. We will wish each other all the happiness we could ever find.

With all my love, Rishat

To her surprise, as tears poured down her face, Emily felt relieved. The idea of bringing Rishat and Jaya to America had been a lot for her to process. She had no realistic concept of how to do this or what the end result might be.

Now, she felt she could have this amazing relationship with a wonderful woman without uprooting everyone's life.

She discovered it is okay to experience the joy of emotional love without acting on the physical desire. The gratification is still rewarding.

Emily didn't feel like she was missing out on anything or that there would be regrets down the road. The relationship they are developing is healthy and fills them both with joy.

She is overjoyed that Rishat is rediscovering her marriage and family relationships.

That is where she needs to be right now, and Emily understands what she is saying. In finding each other, they found their faith in their own way. And she believed.

It will all be for the Glory of God in the end.

Emily wiped her tears and decided to take a minute before replying when the phone began playing Bridge Over Troubled Water.

"Hi, Kurt. What's up?"

Chapter 28 – Jaya

Jaya woke up on Friday morning in her room at university. The sun was shining, and the birds were singing outside her window beside her bed. She glanced at the clock that said 9:30.

She only had one class today, and it wasn't till this afternoon. She had plenty of time and was in no hurry to get up. Besides, the other students on her floor would be waiting in line for the showers.

Why fight the crowd?

She rolled over and saw her roommate packing.

"Are you going home for the weekend?" She asked her.

"Yes. I only have science this morning at 10:00, and then I will drive back to Valsad. My family is having a dinner party on Saturday night for the friends and some neighbors, and I'd like to see some of my old classmates," Sharma said.

Jaya really liked Sharma, they called her by her surname because her first name was long and hard to pronounce, and wished she would stay on campus this weekend. In fact, almost all the first-year students went home on the weekends, leaving the university empty and lonely.

But Jaya went to this school far away from home so she could have her independence and live without her parents looking over her shoulder and telling her what to do. Besides, things had gotten so stressful at home with her mom and dad that she had a hard time being around them.

When Jaya was growing up, both her parents were very loving and close to her, but as time went on, she saw they were growing apart from each other. Now, there's a heaviness in the air when they are together.

Jaya very much enjoyed the vacations she took with them separately and was surprised at how relaxed and fun her mom was with family and friends. But when they traveled together for the Easter celebration in Mumbai, she felt like a buffer between them.

"You are welcome to come and spend the weekend with me at my family's home if you like. You will get to meet some of the friends I went to school with," Sharma said.

"Thank you. But I have a class this afternoon, and I don't want to hold you up."

"Okay. Well, I hope you find something to do for the weekend and don't stay in the room alone the whole time. Just be careful on your own."

"I appreciate you worrying about me. I'll be okay,"

Jaya replied, wishing she could go. She had hoped Sharma would say she would wait but understood why.

Once Sharma left, Jaya got up to get ready for class. The showers had emptied out, and she had the place all to herself. She dressed and went for some coffee and a bite to eat at the campus cafeteria before class.

Beginning Education was one of her favorite classes and she was glad she scheduled it on Friday afternoon. It is her last class of the week, and she looks forward to it and then the weekend.

As she listened to the lecture, her mind wandered to her mother, who had given up her dream of becoming a teacher to raise her. Jaya's father had wanted to arrange for her to marry a teacher at his school instead of going to university. She knew right away she didn't want that and stood her ground.

Jaya knew her mother did not regret her decision. She often told Jaya how grateful she was to be able to do some work from home so she didn't have to leave her. She always called her a blessing, and Jaya felt loved by both her parents.

For some reason, Jaya began to feel homesick. She decided to drive home for the weekend after all. She would leave right after class. It was a five-hour drive, so she would have to pack quickly.

In her room, she hurriedly threw a few items in an overnight bag, jumped in her car, and left. She stopped only once for a coffee and bathroom break. There was not much traffic, and she made it in good time.

When she arrived at her parents' apartment, she entered and saw Cujo lying on the living room floor, looking into the kitchen, panting and wagging his tail. She heard laughter coming from that direction. This was a strange sound, and she wondered if they had company.

When she rounded the corner, she saw her parents, mom with her hands in the sink, and dad holding a dish towel. They were doing the dishes together, playfully splashing each other with soapy water.

When they saw her they looked like two little kids who got caught doing something bad.

"What are you doing here?" Rishat asked her.

"I live here," Jaya said with a chuckle, looking at them like they were strangers.

"What your mother means is we did not expect you home," Kumar said.

"Obviously!" Jaya responded, laughing.

"Are you hungry? Put your things away and come sit down and eat something. We have lots of leftovers from dinner," Rishat said.

"Let me get it for her. You sit down, and the two of you can chat," Kumar said to Rishat.

Jaya couldn't believe what she was seeing. How did this come about? She couldn't wait to hear. Going to her room, she went past their bedroom and stopped in shock.

There, in the middle of her parents' bedroom, was a double bed.

Chapter 29 – Sammy

Drew offered Sammy a place to stay for a few days until he decided what he wanted to do. He took him to Goodwill and got him some extra clothes, paid for out of a stipend at the church for this kind of charity, he told him.

Sammy hated the thought of being considered a 'charity case' but had to admit, in fact, that he was a charity case.

The clothes he picked were actually not too shabby: two pairs of jeans and two shirts. They grabbed a used backpack to keep his stuff in for a couple of bucks.

Drew bought him a pack of underwear at Walmart though he said he didn't need them, and some personal hygiene items of his own so they didn't have to share.

Sammy had managed to keep himself as clean cut as possible since someone in the homeless community always had razors and scissors they dug out of a dumpster somewhere.

Occasionally, a barber in the strip would offer a free shave and hair cut to the homeless for a day, but they didn't always know what that day was until some of the others showed up freshly cut and let them know.

They'd high tail it over but didn't always make it in time, or there was a line around the corner, and he didn't feel like waiting.

Drew went to work every day, leaving Sammy in his house to do what he wanted. He couldn't believe the guy just trusted him like that. A few times, Sammy let anger get to him and thought of just leaving and going off the grid again, but something stopped him. He was tired.

Tired of being homeless, living on the street, under a bridge, beside the river, anywhere but in a home like this, with comfort and security. What was stopping him from going home?

Shame! Guilt!

He was still sending himself those negative messages, thinking that he didn't deserve a better life.

Where is that coming from?

He was angry with Emily for leaving him. That was it! He hadn't recognized it before.

He had to forgive her. She was obviously sorry since she went to all this trouble to find him.

The man said she really wanted to reconcile with me.

He did deserve a better life. He deserved a home. Love. Just like everyone does. At that moment he knew. He decided to go home.

Chapter 30 – Kurt

Friday morning, Kurt came to work to find a message on his machine from Sammy. Since he was running late that day, he had clients waiting for him in the lobby. This would have to wait.

As the day went on, he forgot about the message until he saw Emily in the lounge having lunch. He walked in, looked at her, grabbed his lunch out of the frig, and started to walk out.

"Hey, wait! Where ya going?" she asked, thinking his behavior odd.

"I just thought I'd eat in my office today since I have so much work to catch up on. Not really taking a break. All these cases we took on for Casey have got me all bogged down," he looked at her closely to read her reaction. She wasn't buying it.

"If you need help, I can take some off your hands," she replied.

"No. No. I've started them. I have to stick with them."

"What's going on? I feel like you've been dodging me," they had been avoiding each other off and on since all this with Sammy started.

"Listen, I really do have some stuff to take care of. I'll call you tonight. We'll talk," he bolted out of the room before she had a chance to continue asking questions.

He only had like thirty minutes to eat before his next client came in, and he had no idea if he would reach Sammy or how long that conversation would take.

Back in his office, he picked up his sandwich and the phone simultaneously. While chewing, he dialed the number Sammy had left on his machine. He assumed it was Drew's.

And sure enough, it was.

"Hello," Drew answered.

"Hey, Drew," Kurt said, swallowing quickly. "This is Kurt Holden. I got a message from Sammy this morning."

"He's right here. Hold on," he called out. "Sam! You've got a phone call."

Sammy took the phone, "Hello."

"Hi, Sam. It's Kurt. I got your message this morning. Sorry, this is the first chance I've had to call back."

"That's okay," Sammy said. "I'd like to come see my sister. Drew said he'd bring me. Can you arrange it for me? What should I do?"

"Yes, I can. When can Drew bring you in?"

Sammy asked Drew, "He wants to know when you can bring me in."

"How about tonight?" Drew answered.

"Is tonight okay?" he asked Kurt.

"It sure is. Have Drew bring you here to my office. I think he knows where it is."

"We can be there about 6:00," Drew said to Sammy who repeated to Kurt.

"That'd be good. I look forward to meeting you, Sam," he hung up, contemplating whether he should tell Emily what was happening and how to go about this.

He decided it was best to say nothing right now, just in case Sammy backed out and didn't come.

Kurt had told Emily he'd call her tonight, so he figured she would be home. If, indeed Sammy made it, he would just take him to her house. That sounded like the best plan.

For the rest of the day, Kurt avoided Emily. He did not want to answer questions or show his excitement about finding Sammy and being a part of her reconciliation.

He was overjoyed to be able to bring them together.

He couldn't wait to see her face.

She had been so overwhelmed with emotion over all that was going on in her life. He hoped this would bring calmness back to her.

He didn't know what was going on with the woman in India, and she didn't seem to want to confide that in him, so he had to believe she was making good decisions about it.

Kurt finished up with his last client at 5:00 and had nothing to do for the next hour. He typed up his evaluation and checked on some other clients he was covering for Casey.

Before he knew it, the buzzer from the front desk went off. That meant someone was waiting for him in the lobby. He got up and went out to greet them.

"Hi Sam," he put his hand out to shake with the tall, thin young man in front of him. "I'm Kurt."

Sammy shook his hand.

"And I'm Drew," they shook hands and Kurt invited them to come back into the conference room.

"Can I get you anything to eat or drink?" He asked them. "How about some coffee?"

"Coffee would be great for me," Drew said.

"I'll take a cup, too," said Sammy.

He poured the coffee and put cream and sugar on the table for them, then sat down.

"Sam, I haven't told Emily I have been in touch with you. I wanted to make sure you would come, and I wanted to talk about what to expect with this meeting."

"I understand. How do you know my sister?" Sammy asked, not really knowing anything about this yet. "I was told there is a family situation."

"She is a counselor here, and she has been looking for you for a while. She really wants a reconciliation with you, like I told you on the phone. I was asked to help find you, and I'm overjoyed that I did."

"So, you are coworkers here? She's here? Now?"

"Yes, we are coworkers, but no, she is not here this moment. She has gone home for the day. But at this point, I think I need to bring you two together and let you work it out from here. She is expecting me at her house. I'd like to take you there if that's okay?"

Drew decided to jump in at this point, "Sam. You are not under any pressure here. If you're not ready, we can wait."

Sammy had confided in Drew the last few days, and he knew how Sammy was feeling, about how angry he was that she just left him. He felt abandoned, lost and lonely. He would have a lot of healing to do with her.

"We can let her know where you are. You can talk on the phone at first if that's more comfortable for you. The point is you are in control of all of this. It's your choice."

"There's that word again. Control. I am in control. The choice is mine," he felt overwhelmed with emotion, too. But he wasn't in control because he didn't know how all of this was going to end.

Drew and Kurt sat back quietly to let him work through his thoughts and feelings.

Finally, he decided, "Alright. Take me to my sister."

"Okay. Let me grab my phone and keys. I'll meet you in the lobby," he went to his office, grabbed his things, and locked up.

In the lobby, they walked outside together, but Kurt was parked in the employee lot.

"I'll pull around to the front here and pull over. You can get behind me and follow me."

In the car, he called, "Hi, Emily. Hey, are you home? Can I stop over for a minute? I'd like to talk."

Chapter 31 – The Reconciliation

Emily sat on her patio, waiting for Kurt to arrive. She felt spring in the air and all new things coming to life. The birds continue to build their nest in the vent, preparing to have their babies.

Rishat was building a new relationship with her husband of twenty years, rekindling the love of their youth, and building a complete relationship with her daughter that would be whole and happy.

Their friendship would continue to grow beyond the physical desire to a deeper emotional level that would be fulfilling to both of them. Two women, offering each other support and encouragement through all of life's challenges.

Emily saw Kurt's car come down the road and pull up in front of her house. Another car was behind him.

She got up and walked around the house to see who it was.

From the yard, she could see a tall, thin young man step out of the car behind Kurt. She could not believe her eyes. She barely recognized him, but her heart knew who it was.

And she ran!

Sammy saw her coming but didn't expect the impact as she jumped in his arms. She was sobbing, which triggered his reaction to sob as well.

They stayed that way until, in his weakness, he could no longer hold her up.

Emily's feet hit the ground, but her arms held on tight. She could not let go, and he didn't want her to. He couldn't remember ever being embraced with this much love by anyone.

"I'm sorry. I'm so sorry," she started saying and once again he responded.

"I'm so sorry," he cried and held her tighter.

After a few minutes, they realized they were being watched. Emily let go of Sammy and went to embrace Kurt.

"Oh my gosh. I don't know how this happened, but I can't thank you enough. How will I ever thank you."

Kurt found himself responding with emotion as well, in a different way to what he was used to.

"There's no need. Watching this reunion is thanks enough," he said.

Then he turned to Drew, "This is Drew Mangeli. He's a youth counselor at a church in Pittsburgh. He played a big part in making this happen."

Emily hugged him and said, "Thank you! Would you all like to come in and have some coffee."

The situation then got awkward, and no one knew what to do.

She put her arm around Sammy and led him into the house. The others followed.

In the kitchen, she made them each a fresh cup of coffee from her Keurig, putting out cream and sugar.

They sat and talked about how this all came together.

"It's a miracle," she said and honestly believed it.

"There was a force at work here for sure," Drew said.

As it got late, Drew excused himself, having an hour's drive home and he didn't like driving in the dark much anymore.

It was decided already that Sammy would be staying, so he walked out to the car with Drew to get his backpack.

"I can't thank you enough, Drew," he said. "For everything."

"No need, Sam," Drew hesitated for a minute, then said, "Listen. Once you get on your feet and decide what you want to do with your life, you will always be welcome to come and counsel the other homeless and juvenile boys at the churches and shelters. We really need someone like you, with a success story, to encourage them and get them going in the right direction."

Sammy thought of all the pictures he saw on the walls at the shelter, and he didn't believe any of it at the time. Now he understood.

"That's something to think about. Thanks. I never thought I'd have a future like that in a million years."

"And that's why you'd be good at it," he shook his hand, got in his car, and beeped as he drove off.

When Sammy went back into the house, Emily and Kurt were saying their goodbyes. He shook Kurts's hand again and said, "Thanks again."

"I'm always here, Sam, if you need to talk. Emily's a good counselor, but sometimes a guy needs a guy, ya know."

They all laughed.

Once Kurt left, Emily showed Sammy where everything was. The spare room is now his room. They would shop for some more clothes over the weekend.

When he was settled in, they sat up all night talking and reminiscing, laughing and crying. It was the best time for them. They had a long road ahead of them.

Sammy would get a part time job at the hospital in

housekeeping with Emily's encouragement and Kurt's recommendation. He would also enroll in school, for which the hospital would partially pay.

When Emily arrived at work on Monday morning, she had a bouquet of roses on her desk with a note that said, 'Are you free for dinner sometime? Kurt.'

Emily's heart was full of joy. She had a family and a hopeful future.

She reached over and turned on her radio. Rascal Flatts' methodic melody came across singing *God Bless the Broken Road.*

She smiled. *Ok. Let's see where this goes.*

References

Your Tango, NyRee Ausler, Why You Feel So Lonely but Still Hate Being Around People, October 1, 2023.

Disclosure: Though some of the services are offered, not all information regarding the homeless shelters in Pittsburgh is verified and is fictionally presented by the author for the sake of the story.

Questions for Book Club Discussion

When Rishat didn't write back immediately, did Emily do the right thing to write a second letter?

Did Emily abandon Sammy?

What happened to the dachshund?

Why do you think Sammy was homeless instead of asking Emily for help?

Do you think Sammy has a right to be angry?

Why doesn't the author give us the name of a specific church?

Do you think Emily and Rishat were really in love?

What do you think of delaying or denying physical gratification?

Why did the author not introduce us to Kumar until the end of the book?

What does the author reveal about Jaya's relationship with her parents?

What kind of young man do you think Sammy really is?

Why does Kurt call Sammy 'Sam?'

When did you know Emily and Kurt would get together?